W9-AED-896

Countries and Cultures

by
Ron Wheeler

illustrated by
Tom Heggie

FS-10124 Countries and Cultures
All rights reserved–Printed in the U.S.A.
Copyright © 1994 Frank Schaffer Publications, Inc.
23740 Hawthorne Blvd.
Torrance, CA 90505

Table of Contents

Introduction

The people of the world vary in appearance, clothing, customs, and ideas. They eat different foods and enjoy different traditions. *Countries and Cultures* highlights the various influences—historical, geographic, and cultural—that have formed many of the world's most distinctive cultures.

Countries and Cultures is divided into seven sections, each devoted to one of the following important regions of the world: Europe, the Orient, the Pacific World, the Middle East, Africa, Latin America, and Northern America. Each section begins with an overview, complete with teaching ideas and an up-to-date map of the region, designed to help students see the region from a whole new perspective.

Each of the 37 easy-to-use miniunits in this book focuses on a nation from one of the seven regions. Specifically, each miniunit includes the following elements:

- Concise and interesting information
- Challenging questions for students to investigate
- Practical interdisciplinary teaching ideas that cut across the curriculum
- Two reproducible student activity pages for independent study

This action-packed resource book contains an array of motivational activities that stress important content and skills from social studies, language arts, mathematics, science, art, music and health, as well as other areas like sports, education, and environmental studies.

Countries and Cultures will provide your students with hours of fun while learning basic information about the world. The book includes "hands-on" lessons such as building Egyptian pyramids, weaving Guatemalan blankets, creating Japanese wood block art, learning foreign words, plotting places on maps, and graphing and interpreting data, to list just a few. Your students' reading and writing skills will be enhanced as they participate in innovative activities such as "I Was There: The Fall of the Bastille," "Russia's Czars," "Japanese Festivals," "Colorful Thailand," "Black South African Leaders," "Mayan Civilization," and many, many more.

High technology, jet travel, international trade, and the end of the Cold War have brought the nations of the world closer together. In this new era of global interdependence it is imperative that students gain an understanding and awareness of the whole world, its countries, and its cultures. Your students' ability to succeed in the twenty-first century will depend on the international skills they acquire now.

Europe:

An Overview for the Teacher

Many Americans today can trace their cultural heritage back to Europe. No region of the world has influenced the course of American history more than Europe. European exploration, colonization, and immigration have left an indelible mark on our nation's character, institutions, and values. To introduce the unit, ask students to think about all of the links, both historical and current, between Europe and the United States.

Make a transparency of a political outline map of Europe which shows major mountain ranges and river systems. Invite volunteers to identify various countries and other geographic features on the transparency. Encourage students to share any information they have about the various countries and cultures. Use the following information to give your students an overview of Europe.

Ask students to describe the shape of Europe. Point out to students that Europe is a land of peninsulas. See how many peninsulas students can find on the map. Much of Europe is near the sea. Many major European cities are either located alongside the sea or on rivers that have access to the sea. Historically, some of world's most important centers of commerce and trade were European cities which had direct access to the sea, such as Genoa, Venice, Amsterdam, and London. Ask students to locate some of Europe's major population centers. How many of these centers are on or near the sea? Europe's climate is also influenced by the sea. The winds blowing toward Europe from the Atlantic Ocean have a warming effect on the continent. Most of western Europe has a maritime climate. Southern Europe also has a mild climate which is influenced by the Mediterranean Sea.

Europe has much cultural diversity. The region consists of over 30 countries, including the new nations of the former Soviet Union. There are over 35 languages spoken in Europe. Three major religions (Roman Catholic, the Orthodox Eastern Church, and Protestant) are represented. Recent immigration from Asia and the Middle East has added even more diversity to Europe's population mix. Deep-rooted ethnic and religious tensions (and conflicts) are present today in some parts of Europe. Point out some of the current trouble spots and discuss them briefly with students.

Much of Europe's history is about the nations of Europe fighting among themselves. In the twentieth century, however, two European wars—World Wars I and II—spread to almost every corner of the planet. Today, the nations of Europe are finding ways to work together—ways that will hopefully lead to greater European cooperation and prosperity. The most significant example of European collaboration is the European Community or EC, which is an organization designed to promote free trade among the nations which are members. The EC might be the first step toward a unified and more peaceful Europe.

Europe

Britain

Beautiful landscapes and 2,000 years of history await visitors to the United Kingdom of Great Britain and Northern Ireland. Simply called Britain by most people, this island nation is made up of four lands: England, Wales, Scotland, and Northern Ireland. England, the largest and most populous of the four, is noted for its many famous historic attractions such as Hadrian's Wall (built by the Romans to keep out wild northern tribes), the medieval city of York, the mysterious ruins at Stonehenge, and the university city of Cambridge. Landmarks in England's capital, London, include Buckingham Palace, Westminster Abbey, and the British Museum. Wales, with its own Welsh language, is noted for its numerous festivals, called *eisteddfeds*, which celebrate traditional Welsh culture. Scotland, home of highland dancers and bagpipers, also retains a strong sense of its Scottish identity. Life is not so pleasant in Northern Ireland which is involved in a long and bitter conflict over whether it should remain part of Britain. What continues to hold all of Britain's people together is its government. The British government consists of three parts: the Monarchy and the House of Lords, which have little political power, and the House of Commons, which is the supreme decision-making body. The House of Commons' 650 members are directly elected by voters, and this assembly forms the basis of Britain's democratic system of government. The British parliamentary system has been adopted by many countries around the world.

INVESTIGATIONS

The shield on Britain's official coat of arms is supported by a lion and a unicorn. What do these two animals symbolize?

DIEU ET MON DROIT

What is the name of this world-famous clock in London?

Stratford-upon-Avon was the birthplace of this celebrated playwright and poet. Who was he?

Environmental Studies: Like other industrialized countries, Britain is striving to develop measures to protect the environment from pollution. In small groups of four or five, present students with a problem related to one aspect of pollution in Britain: air (including climate change, acid rain, vehicle emissions, smoke and ozone), water (including hazardous substances and waste, sewage and pollution from ships and farms), and land (including waste disposal and litter). The groups can write proposals setting forth their solutions, drawing on information they have gathered about the geography, history, and economy of Britain.

Government: Although the United States and Britain both have democratic systems of government, the systems are still quite different from each other. British parliamentary democracy is based on political parties competing to form governments. The main political parties are Conservative and Labour. The leader of the party which wins the most seats in the House of Commons, or which has the support of a majority in the House of Commons, is invited by the Monarch to form a government. This person becomes Prime Minister and chooses the ministers who will together form the government. Encourage students to learn more about Britain's two major parties. The chart below shows the number of Conservative and Labour candidates elected to Parliament in the 1970 through 1987 general elections. Can students draw any plausible inferences about British politics from these data? Currently, which political party heads the government? Who is the current Prime Minister?

	1970	1974(Oct)	1974(May)	1979	1983	1987
Conservative	330	297	277	339	397	376
Labour	287	301	319	269	209	229

Science: Some of the world's most famous scientists and inventors were British. In fact, the Industrial Revolution began in Britain with the birth of the textile industry. Ask students to identify a major accomplishment and historical time period for each British scientific thinker and inventor listed below. Then, let them create a time line that shows the times when the events occurred.

Francis Bacon (1605) proposed that scientists should observe nature and test their observations.
Isaac Newton (1687) discovered the law of gravity.
John Kay (1733) invented the flying shuttle.
James Hargreaves (1764) invented the spinning jenny.
James Watt (1769) invented the steam engine
Richard Arkwright (1769) invented the waterframe.
John L. McAdam (1700s) developed a new method to build hard-surface (macadam) roads.
Jethro Tull (1733) invented the seed drill.
George Stephenson (1814) built the first successful steam locomotive.
Charles Darwin (1859) proposed the theory of evolution.

British Government

Unlike most other nations, Britain does not have a single written constitution which describes the form and functions of the government. Instead, the British Constitution and Parliament are based on laws and customs which have evolved over many centuries. Listed below are some statements related to three elements of the British government: the monarchy and the two Houses of Parliament (the House of Lords and the House of Commons). In Britain the monarch can be either a king or queen. Members of the House of Lords and the House of Commons are called MPs (which stands for member of Parliament). Use classroom and library resources to complete the activity below. If the statement is about the Monarch, place an M on the space. If it is about the House of Lords, place an L. If it is about the House of Commons, place a C.

_____ 1. Passes laws

_____ 2. Final court of appeal for laws

_____ 3. Elected by voters

_____ 4. Head of State

_____ 5. Votes on taxes

_____ 6. Non-elected MPs

_____ 7. Awards honors, decorations, and medals

_____ 8. Chooses Prime Minister

_____ 9. Abolishes laws

_____10. Formally approves legislation

_____11. Usually a member of a political party

_____12. Gives speech at the opening of Parliament

_____13. MPs who are archbishops and bishops

_____14. MPs who are peers and peeresses

_____15. Runs for election

The Four Lands of Britain

Although Britain's four lands–England, Wales, Scotland, and Northern Ireland–have many characteristics in common, each also has its own unique history, geography, and culture. Use classroom and library resources to help you match the characteristics listed below with the proper places. Put an *E* for England, *W* for Wales, *S* for Scotland, and *NI* for Northern Ireland in the space provided.

_____ 1. It was defeated at the Battle of Hastings in 1066.

_____ 2. Its people were known as Picts.

_____ 3. It has the most members in the House of Commons.

_____ 4. It has coal fields in Yorkshire.

_____ 5. It is a principality.

_____ 6. Golf was invented here.

_____ 7. Its capital, London, is one of the world's centers for banking, insurance, and manufacturing.

_____ 8. Home of Robert Burns, James Watt, and Adam Smith

_____ 9. Its capital is Belfast.

_____10. Has medieval college in Oxford

_____11. Home of "Nessie," the Loch Ness monster.

_____12. Its capital is Edinburgh.

_____13. Site of Hadrian's Wall

_____14. Its patron saint is St. Andrew.

_____15. Its capital is Cardiff.

_____16. Welsh is an important language here.

_____17. A major city is Glasgow.

_____18. It is smallest in land area.

_____19. It is largest in land area.

_____20. France is directly across the English Channel from it.

Germany

In 1989 Germans jumped for joy when the Berlin Wall, which symbolized the enforced separation of their country, came tumbling down. This historic event ended 44 years of Communist control of East Germany and led to the joining of the two Germanys under the democratic leadership of West Germany. At the time of unification, West Germany was one of the world's richest industrialized countries. East Germany, in comparison, was backward and poor. Today, there are many problems associated with integrating the two very different economic and political systems, but most Germans are happy that the two are one country again. Located in the middle of Europe, Germany is at the center of the continent's economic activity. The nation is noted for its many excellent manufactured products. Some of the best cars in the world, including BMW, Mercedes-Benz and Porsche, are built in Germany. Also well-known are Germany's freeways, called *autobahnen*, which have no speed limits! Germany has a long and rich history. The remains of Roman buildings can be seen today in cities like Augsburg, Trier, and Cologne. Regal castles and magnificent monasteries and churches built during the Middle Ages dot the German landscape.

What is the name of this famous symbol of Berlin?

INVESTIGATIONS

In the sixteenth century this person started a new church in Germany and translated the Bible into German. What was his name?

Some common things in America came from Germany. *Kindergarten* is a German invention. What does the word mean in German?

Music: Today, young people in Germany like much of the same music that young Americans like. However, some of the world's greatest classical music came from Germany. Have students investigate the lives of the following famous German composers: Johann Sebastian Bach, Ludwig van Beethoven, Johannes Brahms, Robert Schumann, Richard Wagner, and Felix Mendelssohn. Encourage your students to listen to these composers' music (some of which might be available in your school or community library or from the music or band teacher). You may also want to let the whole class listen to some of the more popular selections.

Language Arts: English and German languages come from a common source. The German language was brought to Britain by Germanic-speaking tribes around the year A.D. 400. Put the following German words on the chalkboard and ask students to guess the similar English words (which are in parentheses): Wasser (water), Vater (father), Mutter (mother), Pfefferminz (peppermint) and Apfel (apple). Challenge students to find other similar German and English words.

Geography: The first German settlers arrived in America in 1683. Since that time, millions of Germans have come here to live.

Let students use resource books to identify and locate places in the United States where significant numbers of Germans have settled. For example, an estimated one-third of Milwaukee, Wisconsin's 628,088 residents are of German descent. If any of your students are of German descent, let them trace the German origins of their families. On a map of Germany, they can identify the places from which their ancestors came.

History: Assign small groups of four or five students one of the following historical periods to research. After the groups have prepared written reports on their topics, let each group create a brief skit based on its report to present to the class. The historical periods in chronological order follow: Roman Times, Middle Ages, German Empire, Weimar Republic, Third Reich, Cold War and the "New" Germany. Give students plenty of time to prepare and practice their skits. Encourage creativity. They can make period costumes, design sets, and develop colorful dialogue. Give them some examples of scenes they could recreate. A skit about Roman Times might depict a battle in which Julius Caesar defeated the Germanic tribes, or a skit about the "New" Germany might dramatize a scene in which Germans participated in the destruction of the hated Berlin Wall.

Science: Have students research the following German inventors and their inventions: Zeppelin (airship), Bunsen (gas burner), Diesel (diesel engine), Geiger (geiger counter), Daimler (motorcycle), and Gutenberg (movable type).

Traveling Through Germany

Although Germany is much smaller than the United States, its geography is varied and there are many interesting places to see. Below are listed places you might want to visit on a trip to Germany. Find a map of Germany in an atlas or encyclopedia and use it to locate these places. First, on the outline map below, draw and label the following rivers: Rhine, Danube, Moselle, Main, and Elbe. Then write the number that corresponds with each place below to show its correct location on the map.

1. Hamburg
2. Berlin
3. Thuringian Forest
4. Saxony
5. Black Forest
6. Munich
7. Düsseldorf
8. Bonn
9. Frankfurt
10. Dresden
11. Rhineland
12. Bavarian Alps
13. Bohemian Forest
14. Ruhr Valley
15. Saar River
16. Rhineland-Palatinate
17. The North German Plain
18. Heidelberg
19. Cologne
20. Bremen

Name _____

Comparing Germany and the United States

Germany and the United States are similar in many ways; Germans dress much the same as Americans, and German students like the same music and movies that American students enjoy. Some characteristics are different, however. Some characteristics of the German people and Germany are described below on the left. Fill in the corresponding American equivalent in the blank space provided.

In Germany   **In the United States**

People shake hands almost *every* time they meet.   _____

Almost all buildings are made of brick or stone.   _____

If people go to dinner at a friend's house, they
bring flowers for the host.   _____

There are lots of sidewalk cafes.   _____

In cities and towns, houses have no front
yard or only a small one.   _____

Students have six weeks of summer vacation.   _____

Most school children are required to write
with a fountain pen.   _____

Most students learn a foreign language, usually
English.   _____

Many streets are narrow and made of cobblestones.   _____

There are lots of castles.   _____

The school year is 210 days.   _____

Sweden

Just 100 years ago, Sweden was a poor farming country. At that time hundreds of thousands of Swedes, fleeing bad harvests and starvation, went to the United States in search of a better life. Today, Sweden is one of the world's most prosperous industrial countries. Most Swedish workers enjoy five weeks of paid vacation a year. Schooling, including books and meals, health services, and pensions are provided free by the government. All of these services are paid for by taxes, which are very high. Sweden is both a democracy and a monarchy. Swedes vote for people to represent them in the Riksdag (or Parliament), which is the country's highest decision-making body. The nation also has a king, Carl XVI Gustaf, who has little power and whose job is mainly ceremonial. Most Swedes live in southern and central Sweden where industry and fertile land are located. A group of native people, called Lapps, live in sparsely populated northern Sweden. Some Lapps maintain their traditional culture living off their herds of reindeer as they have for centuries. Sweden is an outdoor paradise with approximately 160,000 lakes, 2,000 miles of coastline and 20 national parks. The country's main exports are wood pulp, paper, cars, machinery, chemical products, iron, and steel.

INVESTIGATIONS

This world-renowned Swede, the strongest girl on Earth, is a character created by author Astrid Lindgren. What is her name?

Early inhabitants of Sweden were Scandinavian seafaring raiders who terrorized much of Europe. What were they called?

This Swedish scientist, who invented dynamite, created a prize which is awarded every year to outstanding scientists, writers, and to those who work for peace. What was his name?

Curriculum Connections

Geography: Have students search for geographic similarities between Sweden and the United States. For example, Sweden is located at about the same latitude (Stockholm, 59°N) as Alaska; its land area (173,731) is similar to California's; and its population (8.6 million) is close to Michigan's. Students also can use reference books to compare Sweden's geology, climate, plants and animals, economy, and patterns of settlement with those of the United States.

Physical Education and Health: Sports and exercise are very popular in Sweden. About 2 million Swedes (almost one-fourth the total population) are believed to engage in physical fitness activities on a regular basis. Encourage students to investigate the lives of world-class Swedish athletes such as Bjorn Borg and Mats Wilander in tennis, Ingemar Stenmark in alpine skiing, and Patrick Sjoberg in high jumping. Students also can prepare reports on some of Sweden's more popular sports such as jogging, soccer, tennis, skiing, cycling, and ice hockey.

Advisory: Students can use the following facts and figures about young people in Sweden to compile a list of similarities and differences between themselves and their Swedish counterparts. Basic schooling in Sweden is compulsory and lasts for nine years. The average number of students in a ninth grade class is 25. Students have one teacher until grade seven when they are taught by subject teachers. No grades (marks) are awarded in Swedish schools until grades 8 and 9. In the earlier grades, marks are replaced by personal conferences between teachers and parents. School marks in Sweden are based on a five-point scale, one being the minimum and five the maximum score. It is very common for Swedish students to work while they are in school and during summer and holidays. Music, dancing, reading books, and sports are very popular among students. Among boys aged 7-15 years, 71 percent took part in sporting activities every week outside of school, as did 60 percent of girls in the same age group. Swedish 12- and 13-year-olds devote more than two hours a day to television and video.

Cultural Celebrations: Ask small groups of three or four students to choose one of the following important cultural events in the annual Swedish calendar to research. After they have gathered information on the events, they can create skits about the celebrations and present them to the class. Nobel Day, December 10, is the day the world-famous Nobel prizes are presented. St. Lucia Day on December 13 marks the day when light will return after the long winter darkness. To symbolize this event, it is customary for the daughter in the family to place a crown of candles in her hair and wake everyone up. On Walpurgis Eve, the evening of April 30, bonfires and singing signal the arrival of spring. St. Martin's Day, November 11, marks the end of autumn work and the start of winter activities. Traditionally, roast goose is eaten on this day. Sweden's Christmas and Easter customs are similar to those of the United States.

Swedish Is Spoken Here

The Swedish language is spoken by Sweden's 8.6 million people. Although Swedish is very different from English, some Swedish and English words are similar in their spellings and pronunciations. Try to match the English words listed on the left with the equivalent Swedish words listed on the right.

English		Swedish	
_____	1. good day	a.	ägg
_____	2. family	b.	kaffe
_____	3. mother`	c.	god dag
_____	4. tea	d.	familj
_____	5. yes	e.	fisk
_____	6. cup	f.	isvatten
_____	7. bananas	g.	bananer
_____	8. chocolate	h.	ja
_____	9. eggs	i.	tre
_____	10. good morning	j.	te
_____	11. thank you	k.	nej
_____	12. milk	l.	mamma
_____	13. ice water	m.	nötter
_____	14. credit card	n.	choklad
_____	15. goodbye	o.	mjölk
_____	16. no	p.	kopp
_____	17. coffee	q.	tack
_____	18. nuts	r.	kreditkort
_____	19. three	s.	adjö
_____	20. fish	t.	god morgon

A Swedish Family's Budget

The pie graph shows the percentage of income spent on taxes and various types of goods and services by a typical Swedish family. Use the graph to answer the questions below.

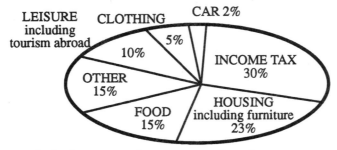

1. Food, housing, and clothing together account for what percentage of a Swedish family's budget? _____

2. What item accounts for the largest percentage of a family's budget? _____

3. What item accounts for the smallest percentage of a family's budget? _____

4. A typical family pays what percentage of its income on clothing? _____

5. What two items account for more than half the budget of a Swedish family? _____
   _____

   If a typical Swedish family's income is $16,000 a year, how much of that income would be spent on the following items?

6. Taxes $_____

7. Leisure $_____

8. Other $_____

9. Car $_____

10. Food and clothing $_____

11. On a separate sheet of paper write a paragraph that compares a Swedish family's budget with a typical American family's.

France

Although perhaps best known for its Eiffel Tower, France is also a nation of varied geography and rich traditions. France's landscape changes from the fertile plains of the north to the majestic Alps Mountains on the Italian border to the sunny Mediterranean seacoast in the south. Mont Blanc in the Alps is the highest point in western Europe at 15,781 feet. Present-day France was called Gaul by the Romans, who conquered it in 52 B.C. After the Franks took control around A.D. 500, Gaul became known as France. The most famous Frankish ruler was Charlemagne, who conquered most of Europe. One of France's national heroines is Joan of Arc. In the fifteenth century this young peasant girl led the French to victory in battle against the English. On July 14, 1789, the French people, to shouts of "liberty, equality, fraternity," stormed the Bastille, an ancient fortress in Paris. This event started the French Revolution and led to the overthrow of King Louis XVI. Today, France is a democratic republic, and its President and Parliament are elected by the people. France hosts 45 million visitors annually, which is more than any other country in the world. France's capital, Paris, is world famous for its art, fashion, and architecture.

What is the name of the train that set a world speed record on May 18, 1991? How fast did it travel?

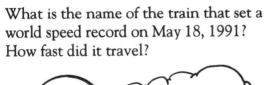

INVESTIGATIONS

This is one of the most popular tourist attractions in Paris. What is it called?

This French woman was burned as a witch by the English. Who was she?

Time Line: France has a long and colorful history. Below are listed some of the more important events and dates in France's past. List the events without the dates in random order on the chalkboard. Ask students to use classroom and library resources to find the dates the events happened. After they have found the dates, they can illustrate the events on white paper and then tape the papers together to show the events in the order in which they occurred. The events and dates in chronological order follow: Charlemagne named Emperor of the Western World (A.D. 800), Louis XIV became King (1643), General Lafayette came to the aid of the American Revolution (1777), French Revolution started (1789), Marie-Antoinette was beheaded (1793), Napoleon Bonaparte became Emperor (1804), France fought Germany in World War I (1914), Germany invaded France in World War II (1939), France was liberated by Allied landing in Normandy (1944), and Francois Mitterrand was elected President of the French Republic (1981). (Note: Your students can create a computer-generated time line with *TimeLiner,* an easy-to-use software program produced by Tom Snyder Productions, 90 Sherman Street, Cambridge, MA 02140. For assistance, contact your school's computer lab teacher.)

Writing: A pen pal program is an excellent way for your students to get to know France and the French people. Students can request French pen pals by writing to the following organization:

Livio Tonso
International Pen Friend Service
256 Via Torino
Ivrea
Italy

Career Education: To give students insight about the international business world, have them consider the following question: What would it be like living in France and working for a French company? Have students create their future business cards. On each card ask them to list three things: job title, job description, and job location. For example, one card might read, *President, Aerospace Industry, Paris;* or *Treasurer, Textile Industry, Lyon.* Ask each student to use reference books to research the locations of various French industries. Some industries now thriving in France include banking, tourism, entertainment, engineering, publishing, transportation, aerospace, education, agriculture, and manufacturing.

A French Feast

The French people are noted for their love of fine food and French cooking is famous around the world. A favorite food of the Gauls was wild boar stuffed with garlic and roasted on a spit. The ancient Gauls also enjoyed snails and goose liver, two delicacies which are extremely popular in France today. French food is very popular in this country, too. Many Americans travel to France to learn the art of French cooking, and there are French restaurants throughout the United States. You probably know more about French food than you think. Try to match the French food terms listed on the left with the equivalent English meanings listed on the right.

French

_____ 1. Au gratin

_____ 2. Baguette

_____ 3. Boeuf Bourguignon

_____ 4. Bouillabaisse

_____ 5. Camembert

_____ 6. Coq au vin

_____ 7. Coquilles St. Jacques

_____ 8. Fines Herbes

_____ 9. Fricassee

_____ 10. Julienne de legumes

_____ 11. Pate

_____ 12. Vichyssoise

_____ 13. Vinaigrette

_____ 14. Escargots

English

A. stewed meat

B. cold soup

C. soft cheese

D. cooked meats served cold

E. topped with cheese

F. fish soup

G. cut vegetables

H. chicken cooked in wine

I. French bread

J. beef stew cooked in red wine

K. scallops cooked in butter served in their shells

L. snails

M. salad dressing

N. herbs

Name _____

The French Revolution

One of the most famous events of the French Revolution was the storming of the Bastille by the people of Paris on July 14, 1789. Bastille Day, July 14, is France's national holiday. The Bastille was the fortress where people critical of King Louis XVI were imprisoned without trial. The Bastille became a symbol of the King's cruel treatment of his people. The winter of 1789 was harsh and long. Food was scarce. The people of France became more and more dissatisfied and restless. They became increasingly angry with the King and his unfair use of power. The peasants, who were among France's poorest people, were especially upset. They wanted opportunities for work and better living conditions. Some excerpts from the journal of a person who witnessed the stormy first days of the French Revolution follow. In the space provided below, use the eye-witness account, as well as other sources, to write your own imaginary account of the storming of the Bastille from the point of view of one of the participants.

July 12   "Angry groups of people begin forming in Paris. Small skirmishes take place. During the night several protest fires are started."

July 13   "Hungry people in Paris search the city for food. They loot the St. Lazare Convent where wheat is stored. During the night more violence breaks out and several gunsmiths' shops are raided."

July 14   "The Bastille prison is stormed. At 5 a.m. the people raid the armory at the Invalides to obtain weapons to defend themselves against soldiers. They take 32,000 rifles and 20 cannons . . . . Once inside the Bastille, the people freed all the prisoners."

July 15   "The people destroy the Bastille. I took a stone from the demolished prison with me as a souvenir of this glorious day."

I Was There: The Fall of the Bastille

_____

_____

_____

_____

_____

_____

Greece

Western civilization—and with it many of the basic freedoms we take for granted—began in Greek city-states over 2,500 years ago. Ordinary people in the ancient world had few rights and no voice in their government. But around 500 B.C. the Greeks came up with a new way to rule. We call this new form of government *democracy*, a word that comes from the Greek words *demos* and *kratos*, which together mean "rule of the people." Of the Greek city-states that had democratic governments, the most important was Athens. Athens was the home of three of the world's most famous thinkers: Plato, Socrates, and Aristotle. The city was also the center of Greek religious and cultural life. Today, the ruins of ancient Athens—the Acropolis and Temple of Zeus—stand among the modern buildings of a busy industrial center of over three million people. Greece is a land of profuse peninsulas, beautiful islands, and rugged mountains. The country's major economic activities include tourism, agriculture, food-processing, manufacturing, and shipping.

This famous temple symbolizes the splendor and glory of ancient Greece. What is it called?

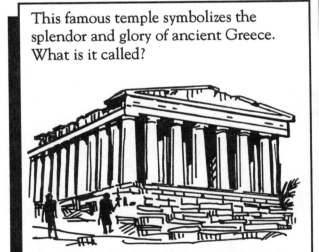

INVESTIGATIONS

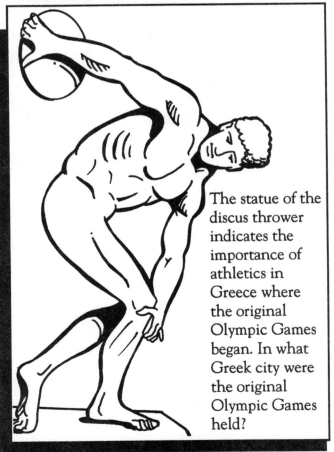

The statue of the discus thrower indicates the importance of athletics in Greece where the original Olympic Games began. In what Greek city were the original Olympic Games held?

Mikonos is one of the many picturesque Greek islands that dot this sea. What is the name of the sea?

History: Historians call the period between about 480 and 399 B.C. "The Golden Age of Greece" because during this time Greek power and culture were at their zenith. Assign students the task of investigating one of the following aspects of ancient Greece's Golden Age: trade, military strength, architecture, philosophy, art, music, politics, and science. The Peloponnesian Wars (431-404 B.C.) between the two most powerful city-states, Athens and Sparta, tore ancient Greece apart. Ask interested students to compare the very different ways of life of these two rival cities. In which of the two cities would students have preferred to live?

Art: For more than a 1,000 years Greece was under the domination of the Byzantine Empire. The emperors of the Byzantine Empire also headed the Christian church, and they worked resolutely to further the spread of Christianity. Inspired by their Christian faith, Greek artists created beautiful Byzantine art in the form of mosaics, wall paintings, and religious objects. After students have gathered background information on Byzantine art, they can make their own Byzantine mosaics. Before they begin, point out that Byzantine mosaics were made from small pieces of stone or glass and that they usually depicted religious persons and important patrons, although scenes or figures, like the "bird in the cage" pavement mosaic shown here, sometimes had no direct connection with the church. The directions for creating the mosaics are as follows:

1. Make a simple sketch of a scene or figure on construction paper. Decide on colors to be used.

2. Tear colored construction paper into 1/2 inch pieces.

3. Arrange the pieces of paper on the sketch.

4. Glue the pieces of paper on the sketch.

Writing: Have each student write a description of his/her mosaic on an index card. Encourage students to make their descriptions as detailed as possible. Collect the mosaics and display them in the classroom. Then, collect, shuffle, and randomly distribute a card to each student, making certain no one gets his/her own card. Challenge students to correctly match the descriptions and the mosaics.

Name _____

The Gods of the Ancient Greeks

The people of ancient Greece had many gods. They included gods of music, war, and wisdom. The Greeks created many myths, or imaginary stories, about the gods which provided explanations for things that happened in the real world. These myths became the basis for Greek art, poetry, music, and theater. For example, Homer's epic poem, the *Iliad*, is based upon a collection of myths about what happens when the Greek god Apollo interferes with the plans of humans. Use your research skills to match the Greek gods on the right with their roles on the left. Put the letter in the blank space.

Role

_____ 1. Avengers of evildoing
_____ 2. Goddess of youth
_____ 3. Father of Zeus
_____ 4. God of fire
_____ 5. God of war
_____ 6. God of the dead
_____ 7. Goddess of motherhood
_____ 8. Goddess of wisdom
_____ 9. Supreme ruler of the gods
_____ 10. Goddess of hunting
_____ 11. God of poetry, music, and prophecy
_____ 12. Goddess of beauty and love
_____ 13. Goddess of agriculture
_____ 14. Goddess of the rainbow
_____ 15. God of the sea
_____ 16. Queen of the underworld
_____ 17. Mother of Achilles
_____ 18. Messenger of the Gods
_____ 19. God of love

Greek god

A. Hermes
B. Zeus
C. Poseidon
D. Iris
E. Apollo
F. Demeter
G. Aphrodite
H. Eros

I. Thetis
J. Hades
K. Cronus
L. Hera
M. Athena
N. Ares
O. Artemis
P. Hephaestus
Q. Persephone
R. Erinyes
S. Hebe

Greek Word Search

Use your research skills to answer the questions about Greece. Write the answers on a separate sheet of paper. Next, find these same words inside the word puzzle. These words can be found horizontally, vertically, diagonally, and sometimes reading backwards. Circle the words.

Clues for Word Search

1. Greece's climate
2. Geographic term describing Greece
3. Greece was the birthplace of this type of government.
4. Traditional Greek musical instrument
5. Greece's largest university
6. Greece's official religion
7. Popular Greek food made with eggplant and meat
8. Greece's most important export
9. This Muslim empire once controlled Greece.
10. The ancient Greek gods lived on this mountain.
11. Born in Greece, but lived and painted in Spain
12. Greek money
13. The island home of Ulysses
14. Greece's most important holiday
15. Largest city in Greece
16. This cooking oil is widely used in Greece.
17. This island is part of Greece.
18. First letter of Greek alphabet
19. Small harplike instrument played by ancient Greeks
20. Greece's flag is white and _____.

```
Q L O B U K L I C U X E C H S O A P X
A N Y T O B A C C O J F L G U Q K T B
L M U Z O G V D T X A K I N O L A S Z
S N H S S P I Q H B S E K Y Z A S L Q
O W O C P W G H Z O K T W M Y B S B W
O N B K A L U S N I N E P B C K U S O
L M D N B R Z R W J A R G L A K O T F
H O H E X C D L Y R E C M U R A M D M
F J L E Z D I V N M N O L E C T C Q S
L A E K M Q F Q F Z A X J X O Z W B P
P J O F O U E E D I R Z Y H M M V X K
S C H F H D S Q Q T R O G S E Z Q F T
Z E W A L Y P S N F E T A Y D S H S W
V L R F U B F P U V T T C M S I L H S
U X O N S D L T Y H I O A I P K M Q U
Q O B F B A D S Z E D M H U K U I K P
Y D L C E F A P J R E A T V H O I D M
E O C I K Y L J I F M N I A C Z D R Y
A H P J V T P X F A O H I E R U S B L
S T P P E E H W P A X P R Z Z O X G O
T R X M I U A A E L I G M M S B K F R
E O P W U K A G Q F L E W K S J J V P
R C R H O B N B Y E A R G Z N G G B B
D Q E P M K E A U I I E U A E N Y L J
L B B R O N B X F Y A S N G H M N L D
M I T R W M O C W G Y W E J T D R N X
E R I A L O F V X Z K W D H A D X R U
```

Italy

Take Alpine slopes, add ancient cities and sunny beaches, and you will have Italy, a boot-shaped land jutting from southern Europe into the Mediterranean Sea. The country's mild climate and natural beauty make it a popular tourist destination. Italy also has a rich history. Some 2,000 years ago, Italy's largest city and capital, Rome, was the center of a huge empire which stretched from the British Isles to Egypt. The ruins of Roman buildings, walls, aqueducts, and highways give us a glimpse today of the Romans' splendid architectural and engineering accomplishments. Prominent among them are the Colosseum, a huge outdoor arena where gladiators once fought to the death; and the Appian Way, an ancient highway between Rome and Brindisi that is still in use. During the Renaissance, Italian city-states like Florence, Genoa, and Venice became important centers of European culture and trade. Today, much of the nation's industrial activity and wealth are concentrated in northern Italy and in Rome, which is in central Italy. Less-prosperous southern Italy is mainly a farming region.

INVESTIGATIONS

This building was built by the ancient Romans as a temple in honor of their gods. What is the building called?

One of the world's largest churches, St. Peter's, is located in an independent state which is completely surrounded by the city of Rome. What is the name of the state?

This city was built on about 120 islands in the Adriatic Sea, and its inhabitants use canals and boats for transportation. What is the city's name?

Language Arts: Although Latin is not spoken today, it is closely associated with many modern languages, including English. In fact, approximately 50 percent of English words are derived from this language spoken by the ancient Romans. For example, the English word *equal* comes from the Latin word *aequalis*. The word *school* comes from the Latin word *schola*. The study of the origins of words is called *etymology*. Challenge students to be etymologists, and let them use dictionaries to find as many English words as they can derived from Latin (most dictionaries include infor-mation about the origin of words). After students have gathered lists of English/Latin words, they can use the information to play a game. To prepare the game, pass out sets of blank index cards to students. Then for each word they find, let them write down the English form of the word on one side of the card and the Latin form on the other side. Next, collect all of the cards and check them for accuracy. After you randomly divide the class into two teams, you are ready to start the game. First, hold up one of the cards so that the class can see the Latin form. Then call on student from one of the teams to tell you the English form. Repeat the process with a student from the other team and continue taking turns until all of the students on both teams have had a turn. Each time a student gives the correct English form, that student's team gets one point. The team that gets the most points wins.

Health and Diet: Italian food is very popular in the United States. In fact, one of America's most liked foods, pizza, came from Italy originally. Encourage students to investigate the Italian food section in the supermarket. They can make a list of the different kinds of pastas, sauces, soups, vegetables, and other foods they find there. How many different foods with Italian names can they find? Most Italian meals include pasta. Students can check the labels to determine ingredients and nutritional values of pastas, as well as other foods. Some students might want to share with the class a favorite Italian recipe from home. Bring Italian cookbooks to class and share them with interested students. Let students check how many of the following traditional Italian ingredients are included in the recipes: olive oil, tomato, cheese, rice, pork, veal, fish, fresh fruit, and wine. Students can also compare the different kinds of restaurants found in the Yellow Pages in the local phone book. Are there more or fewer Italian restaurants than other types? A great way to conclude the students' study of Italian foods is with an assortment of antipasto and pizza squares. Antipasto are bite-sized Italian appetizers consisting of cold meats, vegetables, and olives.

Art: Some of the world's greatest works of art were created by Italians. Introduce students to some of the major works of Leonardo da Vinci, Michelangelo, Raphael, and Titian. Check the school's or community's library for books, posters, and filmstrips displaying these artists' sculpture and paintings.

The Roman Empire

The map below shows the lands bordering the Mediterranean Sea. Between 275 B.C. and A.D. 117, Rome expanded its rule over the area and increased the size of its empire. Use reference sources to do the following: draw a boundary line to show the extent of the Roman Empire at the time of its greatest size and locate and label Rome, Italy, Spain, Britain, Gaul, Corsica, Sardinia, Sicily, Illyria, Dacia, Macedonia, Greece, Crete, Cyprus, Armenia, Mesopotamia, Syria, Judea, Egypt, Carthage, Mauretania, and the Mediterranean Sea. On a separate sheet of paper, answer this question: Why did the Romans continue to expand their empire? Use library resources to help you find as many reasons as you can.

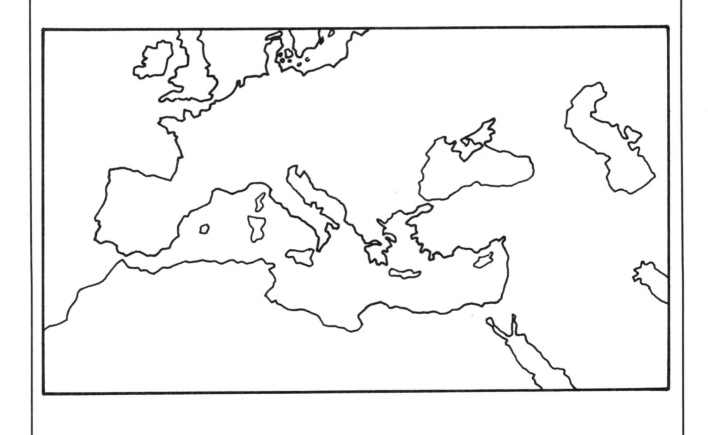

All About Italy

Use your research skills to find answers to this crossword puzzle about Italy.

Across

3. Body of water at sole of boot
4. Birthplace of Christopher Columbus
6. Leader of Italy during WW II
7. Italy is slightly larger than this U.S. state
10. Trained warriors
13. Italian money
15. Italian dish
16. Great Roman poet
17. Roman conqueror of Gaul
18. Romans copied these people

Down

1. Major religion of Italy
2. Roman garment
5. Mountains in Italy
6. Great Italian painter
8. Italian car
9. River in Italy
11. Structures that carried water
12. Type of government in Italy
13. Language of Romans
14. Great Roman orator

Russia

For 75 years Russia and the other 14 republics of the former Soviet Union were under Communist Party rule and closed to foreigners. After the Soviet Union's collapse in 1991, Russia emerged as an independent state. Russia's future is uncertain. The years under communism left the country in chaos. Today, Russians face severe food shortages, unemployment, and pollution. There is reason for hope, however. The world's largest country is blessed with an abundance of natural resources. Russia has huge reserves of coal, iron ore, copper, and oil, as well as extensive forests and farm land. Russia's rich heritage and cultural landmarks are drawing increasing numbers of tourists. In Moscow, the capital and largest city, they come to see Red Square, the Kremlin, and the Bolshoi Theater. In the nation's second biggest city, St. Petersburg, they can visit the spectacular palaces of the Russian *czars* (rulers). Visitors can also cruise more than 1,000 miles of Russia's Volga River and waterways or travel the Trans-Siberian Railroad across two continents between Moscow in Europe and Vladivostok in Asia.

Considered to be one of Russia's greatest writers, this person wrote the novel *War and Peace* in 1869. What was his name?

INVESTIGATIONS

What is the name of this famous Russian Orthodox church in Moscow?

One of Russia's largest cities was named for the same ruler who built this magnificent palace there. What is the name of the city and who was the ruler?

Russia's Czars

During the years from 1547 to 1917, the rulers of Russia were called czars. Short descriptions of the lives of two of Russia's most famous czars are presented below. After you read about the czars, answer the questions that follow on a separate sheet of paper.

Ivan the Terrible

Ivan the Terrible richly deserved his nickname. During his reign (1547-1584) he terrorized his own people and fought neighboring leaders to acquire more territory. He murdered those who disagreed with him, burned whole villages to the ground, and stabbed his own son to death in the middle of an argument. Ivan's army included groups of adventurers and outlaws called *Cossacks*. Skilled horsemen and courageous fighters, Cossacks were feared wherever they rode. Ivan created laws that forced great numbers of poor farmers into bondage to rich landowners. These *serfs*, as they were called, were bound to the land like slaves and lived miserable lives. When Ivan died, he left Russia in turmoil.

Peter the Great

During Peter the Great's rule (1682-1725) Russia underwent tremendous change. Peter greatly admired the ways the more advanced nations of western Europe, such as Germany, England, and Holland, did things. He studied these nations' customs, technologies, and governments. Then he tried to overhaul Russia's ancient society along modern Western lines. To reach his goal, practically no part of Russian life was ignored. Peter even went so far as to force his people to discard their traditional clothing and dress like Germans! He also Westernized the Russian Army and created the Russian Navy. Peter's reign was not peaceful. He gained more territory for Russia after a long war with Sweden. Knowing his efforts to modernize his country would never succeed unless its people were educated, Peter also tried to organize a nationwide school system.

1. Compare and contrast the lives of Ivan the Great and Peter the Great.

2. If you were a Russian, which ruler would you have preferred, Ivan or Peter? Why?

3. Russia's last czar was Nicholas II. Use library sources to research his life. Then, on a separate sheet of paper, write a brief biography of Nicholas. How did his life compare with Ivan's and Peter's?

Spain

Spain is a country of contrasts. There is the old: Roman ruins, Arab fortresses, medieval cathedrals, time-worn rural villages with central plazas, and poor farmers who work the rugged and dry land as they have for centuries. There is the modern: bustling places like Madrid, Spain's capital and largest city, and Barcelona, the nation's leading port and industrial center. Madrid is located on a high plateau, called the Meseta, in the center of Spain. The Meseta is almost entirely surrounded by mountains. Southern Spain's sunny and sandy Mediterranean coast is a popular tourist destination. Other major tourist attractions include El Greco's home in Toledo, Madrid's Royal Palace and Prado Museum, Cordoba's and Seville's cathedrals, and Granada's Alhambra Palace. Around 500 years ago Spain was one of the most powerful nations in the world. The Spanish monarchs, Queen Isabella and King Ferdinand, supported Christopher Columbus' historic voyages. Through the exploration and conquest of the New World, Spain gained vast wealth and a colonial empire. In 1588, after Spain's fleet of warships, called the Spanish Armada, was defeated by the British Navy, Spain began its decline as a world power.

Spain is world famous for this traditional dance which is accompanied by guitar. What is the dance called?

INVESTIGATIONS

In the book, *Don Quixote*, a foolish old man who thought he was a knight rode among white windmills. Who was the author of this Spanish literary classic?

In 1992 the Summer Olympic Games were held in this Mediterranean city. Name the city.

Social Science: One of Spain's most successful sixteenth-century explorers was Hernando Cortés. In 1519 Cortés arrived in present-day Mexico with some 550 men, 16 horses, and 14 cannons. Before long, Cortés would overthrow the powerful Aztec ruler, Montezuma, and gain control over the people of his great Aztec Empire. Students can use library resources to learn more about Cortés' journey. Encourage them to write journals that retrace his path of conquest. Some other Spanish explorers students can investigate are as follows: Francisco Pizarro, conqueror of Peru; Vasco de Balboa, discoverer of the Pacific Ocean; Pedro de Alvarado, conqueror of Guatemala; Juan Ponce de Leon, discoverer of Florida; Hernando de Soto, discoverer of the Mississippi River; and Francisco Vasquez de Coronado, explorer of the southwestern United States.

Foreign Language: Spanish is spoken by 100-300 million people worldwide, and it is the official language of 20 nations, territories, and colonies. Spanish is also spoken by a significant segment of the U.S. population. Have students use library resources to identify and locate Spanish-speaking places around the world and within the United States. Encourage students who speak Spanish to teach the class some simple Spanish words and phrases.

Religion: Spain's population is 99 percent Catholic, which is the largest Christian sect in the world. It was sixteenth-century Spanish and Portuguese explorers and colonizers who brought Catholicism to the native people of Latin America. Have interested students research the history and practice of the Catholic Church. They can report their findings to the class.

Sports and Mathematics: The 1992 summer Olympic Games were held at Barcelona, Spain. Have students make a bar graph of the Olympic medal count for the top nations using the following information: Unified Team (112 total medals), United States (108), Germany (82), China (54), Cuba (31), Hungary (30), South Korea (29), France (29), Australia (27), Spain (22), Japan (22), and Britain (20).

Cultures: Two ethnic groups in Spain that want to maintain their separate languages and cultures are the Catalonians and Basques. Have interested students investigate the history and culture of these groups.

Geography: Let students research one of the following major Spanish cities: Madrid, Barcelona, Valencia, Seville, Toledo, Cordoba, Avila, Granada, or Saragossa.

Historic Spain

Spain's history is long and rich. Use your research skills to match these people, places, and events to learn some facts about Spain. Put the letters on the right in the blanks by the proper numbers on the left.

_____ 1. Spain is part of this peninsula.

_____ 2. They conquered Spain in the early A.D. 700s.

_____ 3. Leader of Spanish Civil War against the government

_____ 4. Spain's major religion

_____ 5. This court brought heretics to trial.

_____ 6. The last of the Moorish states in Spain

_____ 7. The mountains that separate Spain and France

_____ 8. Became king of Spain in 1975

_____ 9. Ethnic group that wants independence from Spain

_____ 10. Spain's largest Moorish palace

_____ 11. Spain wants Britain to return this place.

_____ 12. This nation is separated from Spain by about eight miles of water.

_____ 13. An important forest product

_____ 14. The United States took this island from Spain.

_____ 15. A famous Spanish painter

_____ 16. These people conquered Spain in about 200 B.C.

_____ 17. A Spanish possession

A. Pyrenees
B. Cork
C. Alhambra
D. Romans
E. Iberian
F. Basques
G. Picasso
H. Franco
I. Morocco
J. Moors
K. Cuba
L. Canary Islands
M. Catholic
N. Carlos
O. Inquisition
P. Gibraltar
Q. Granada

Name _____

The Admiral of the Ocean

Although born in Italy, Christopher Columbus' fame was destine to be forever linked with Spain. For it was Spain, under the monarchy of Queen Isabella and King Ferdinand, that gave Columbus the ships, crew, and supplies to try to go where no European had sailed before. Would you have liked to have been among the crew that fateful day, October 12, 1492, when a lookout scanning the horizon first caught sight of the New World? Use library resources to research Columbus' voyages to the New World. Then, imagine you were a member of the crew, and in the space below write a journal documenting your travels and your experiences. Try to incorporate answers to the following questions into your journal: Why did Columbus want to sail across the Atlantic Ocean? Was Columbus' geographic knowledge accurate? Did Columbus' crew believe they would find land? With what peoples and places did Columbus make contact on his voyages? What kind of reception did Columbus get when he returned to Spain?

The Orient:

An Overview for the Teacher

The Orient covers a vast landscape. It includes the ancient countries of China, Mongolia, Korea, and Japan, newly independent nations of the former Soviet Union, the nations of Southeast Asia, the Indonesian archipelago, the subcontinent of India, the Himalayan kingdoms of Nepal and Bhutan, the Moslem republics of Afghanistan, Pakistan and Bangladesh, and the island nation of Sri Lanka. Much of the world's population lives in the Orient. Three of the world's four most populous countries—China, India and Indonesia—are in the Orient. Make a transparency of the political outline map of the Orient on the next page. Ask students to identify various countries and other geographic features on the transparency. Encourage students to share any information they have about the various countries and cultures.

Historically, U.S. laws have either excluded or severely restricted immigration to America from the Orient. People from the Orient first began coming to the United States in the nineteenth century. In the mid-1800s Chinese immigrants arrived in California where they worked as unskilled laborers. Many Chinese were involved with the construction of the Union Pacific Railroad. By 1882, around 375,000 Chinese had entered the United States. Japanese immigrants also entered California during this period. As a result of new immigration policies enacted in the 1960s, the numbers of people from the Orient entering the United States have increased sharply. Between 1985 and 1990, almost 38 percent of the total immigrants to America were Asian. Included among the top 10 nations sending immigrants to the United States in the 1980s, were the Philippines, China, Korea, Vietnam, and India. The influx of new immigrants from the Orient, along with other non-European immigration, is changing the ethnic composition of America, and this impact should continue into the future.

The Orient was once considered distant and mysterious, but now global communications, rapid transportation, and international trade have made the Orient seem as close and familiar as Omaha. Most nations of the Orient, because of their low per capita gross national product (GNP), are called developing countries. Some of the world's poorest countries, such as Bangladesh ($180 per capita) and Afghanistan ($220 per capita), are in the Orient. Today, many of the nations of the Orient are creating a better future for themselves. Japan has emerged from the devastation of World War II to become a world economic power. In the twenty-first century, China, with its huge population, might follow in Japan's economic footsteps. South Korea's booming economy is another Oriental success story. To these three can be added newly industrialized countries like Taiwan, Singapore, Malaysia, and Thailand. Perhaps Indonesia and India might also join this group in the not-too-distant future.

American lives are being affected increasingly by people and events half a world away. Before the students begin their study of this section, explore with them all of the economic, political, historical, and personal connections between the United States and the Orient.

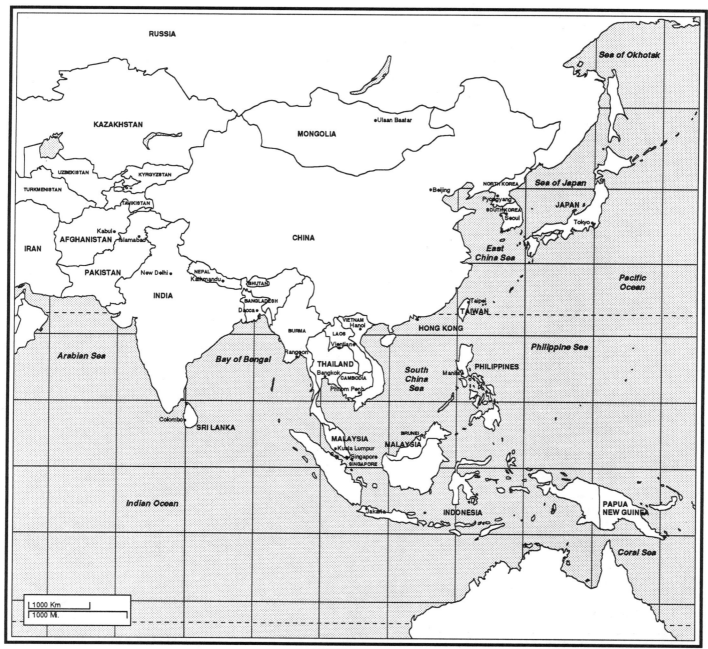

The
Orient

36

India

With a population nearing 900 million, India has the distinction of being the world's largest democracy. India is also one of the oldest and most complex civilizations in the world. About 3,500 years ago Aryan tribes invaded northern India and conquered the Dravidians who then lived there. The Aryans developed Hinduism, which became the major religion of India. Buddhism, founded by Buddha in India in around 500 B.C., influenced Indian religious practices and eventually spread across Asia. In the eighth century A.D. Arab invaders introduced the Islamic religion to the sub-continent. In the seventeenth century Britain established a foothold in India, which became its most important colony. The British built railroads, established schools, and introduced Western ideas, but their economic policies often harmed the Indian people. British rule ended in 1947 when India became an independent nation. Although economic progress has brought prosperity to some Indians, the country continues to face grave problems. These include deep-rooted ethnic and religious conflicts, overpopulation, illiteracy, and widespread poverty.

What was the name of this famous person who led India's non-violent struggle for independence from Great Britain?

INVESTIGATIONS

The god Vishnu is worshipped by Indians who practice India's largest religion. What is the name of the religion?

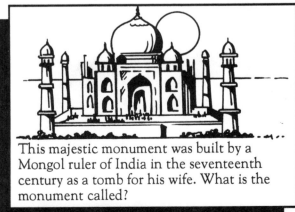

This majestic monument was built by a Mongol ruler of India in the seventeenth century as a tomb for his wife. What is the monument called?

```
                    ▽
        Curriculum
        Connections
```

Music/Dance: For centuries, Indians have used music and dance to express their deep feelings about their culture. These performing arts play an important role in many Indian festivals, and they are often prominently featured in popular Indian films. India's music sounds strange to most Americans' ears. That is because the chords and harmonies found in Western music are absent, and the scale is completely different. Indian song and dance are usually accompanied by stringed instruments and drums. One of the world's best-known Indian musicians is Ravi Shankar. He plays *raga*, or Indian classical music, on a stringed instrument called a *sitar*. Highly exuberant Indian dancers use their arms, hands, and fingers to tell stories and express feelings. Your media center or music teacher can help you locate some tapes of Indian music and dance. After you share some examples of Indian music and dance with students, encourage interested students to investigate the topic further.

Art: Traditional Indian art has been influenced strongly by religious themes. One striking architectural example is the towering Hindu temples in Madras with their intricately carved outer walls. Another is the Taj Mahal, pictured on the preceding page. This exquisite example of India's Islamic architectural style is considered by many to be the most beautiful monument ever created by human hands. Traditional Indian wall paintings were inspired by Buddhism, and Hindu legends were the main subject of colorful Indian miniature paintings. Provide students with examples of Indian art (which can be found in large-page illustrated art books from the school or community library). Encourage interested students to gather more examples, which then can be displayed in the classroom.

Science/Geography: Many scientists believe that plate tectonic theory helps explain the history of the earth. According to this theory, the earth's crust is divided into moving plates. The movement of these plates over millions of years is what caused the present shape and arrangement of the continents. When plates crashed into one another, they formed mountains. It is thought that India and the main continent of Asia were once separate. When India collided with Asia, the Himalayan Mountains were formed. Let students research plate tectonic theory. They can make models and maps which show the arrangement of the earth's land forms at various points in time over the past 200 million years. Since the earth's plates are still moving, challenge students to predict how the earth might look in the very distant future.

Language Arts: Let students work in small cooperative groups of five or six students to create travel folders about India. Students can pick a topic to research from the following categories: history, people, climate, special attractions, geography, and transportation. Encourage students to include colorful illustrations in the travel folders.

Name _____

Interesting India

Amaze your friends with your knowledge of interesting facts about India. Use your research skills to find answers to this crossword puzzle. After you have completed the puzzle, do some more research and create your own crossword puzzle on India for your friends to solve.

Across

5. Huge plateau in India
6. Hindu god
9. Indian breads
12. A group of Indian people who are discriminated against
13. Traditional musical instrument
14. Led the people of India to independence

Down

1. Basic unit of Indian money
2. Hindus believe these animals are sacred
3. Seasonal winds that bring heavy rains
4. Borders India
7. Mountains in northern India
8. Important Indian-made product
9. Spicy Indian food
10. Buddha means this
11. Major industrial center
13. Traditional dress worn by Indian women

India's Many Languages

Hindi, English, and 14 other official languages are spoken in India. Hindi, the national language, and English, the language of business and trade, are the most widely spoken. There are more than a thousand minor languages and dialects. Below is a list of 13 major Indian languages. Use an encyclopedia or other library resource to research the languages and to locate where in India they are spoken. Then indicate on the outline map of India below the location of each of the languages by identifying it by its number.

1. Tamil
2. Hindi
3. Assamese
4. Marathi
5. Kashmiri
6. Teluga
7. Gujarati
8. Oriya
9. Punjabi
10. Malayalam
11. Rajasthani
12. Kannada
13. Bengali

China

With the largest population of any nation on Earth, a land area bigger than the United States, and a history that spans over 4,000 years, China is one of the most important countries in the world. China's capital, Beijing, is in northern China, which is the region where China's culture began. Southern China's mild climate and monsoon rains help make it the country's major agricultural region, with rice the most important crop. In western China is the region of Tibet, which borders the Himalayas, the world's highest mountains. China's huge size and regional differences help explain the cultural diversity found in China; the nation's 1.2 billion people represent a rich variety of ethnic and language groups. For the past 45 years, the ruling Communist Party has held the country together by military force. But many Chinese, who want individual rights and democracy, are now making the Communist leaders feel uneasy. Today, the world waits to see if freedom becomes a part of China's future.

Construction of the Great Wall of China began in 214 B.C. The wall served as a defense against northern invaders. How long is the Great Wall?

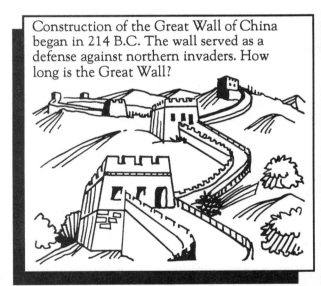

INVESTIGATIONS

This ancient Chinese philosopher's ideas about the ways people and government should act have guided Chinese behavior for centuries. What was his name?

In 1997 this major Asian city will return to Chinese rule. What is the city's name?

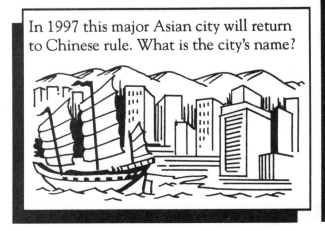

```
         ╲━━━━━━━━━━━━━━━━━━╱
          ╲  Curriculum    ╱
  ━━━━━━━━━━╲ Connections  ╱━━━━━━━━━━
            ╲            ╱
             ╲━━━━━━━━╱
                ╲    ╱
                 ╲  ╱
                  ╲╱
```

Culture/Math: The United States uses the Gregorian Calendar, which was devised in 1582, to measure time. The Chinese use a different calendar that is some 4,000 years old. Like our calendar, the Chinese calendar is based on the phases of the moon, and it is 12 months long. But unlike our calendar, each year in the Chinese calendar is associated with one of 12 different animals. After 11 years, the cycle is repeated again with the same animals in the same order. The first animal in the cycle is the rat. The year of the rat is in 1996. The order for the other 11 animals (with years in parenthesis) follows: ox (1997), tiger (1998), hare (1999), dragon (2000), snake (2001), horse (2002), sheep (2003), monkey (2004), rooster (2005), dog (1994, 2006) and pig (1995, 2007). Traditionally, a person's character and future were linked to his or her birth year and the animal with which it was associated. Let students identify the personal qualities linked to the animals associated with their birth years. Chinese New Year is celebrated between January 20 and February 20 of each year. Have interested students research the way this important holiday is celebrated by the Chinese, as well as by Chinese Americans. If some of your students celebrate the holiday, let them describe the festivities to the class.

History: Before the Republic of China was established in 1912, China was ruled by a succession of dynasties that date back to 1766 B.C. Each dynasty was named after the family or group that maintained power for several generations. Put the names of China's dynasties on the chalkboard. Give each student eight large index cards (one for each dynasty) and a long string from which to hang them. Assign students the task of making a time line from the materials which includes the following information for each dynasty: name, dates, and an important achievement or event with which it was associated. The following dynasties should be placed in correct chronological order on the time line: Shang (1766-1122 B.C.), Zhou (1122-256 B.C.), Qin (221-206 B.C.), Han (202 B.C.-A.D. 220), Tang (618-907), Song (960-1279), Mongols or Yuan (1279-1368), Ming (1368-1644) and Manchus or Qing (1644-1912). Students can display the completed time lines on the walls.

Language Arts: During the Yuan Dynasty, a 21-year-old man from Venice, Italy named Marco Polo journeyed to China. During his long stay there, he became a trusted friend of the great Yuan ruler, Kublai Khan, and he was allowed to travel throughout the empire. After Marco Polo returned to Italy, he described his adventures to a man named Rustichello, who then wrote a book about them. The book was very popular, because Europeans were eager to learn about all the wondrous things that Marco Polo did and saw. Among other things, they were awestruck by such Chinese inventions as gun powder, the magnetic compass, movable type for print, and paper money. Ask students to imagine that they were Rustichello. After students investigate Marco Polo's life, have them write a brief account of his adventures as they might have been told to them by Marco Polo himself.

China's Long History

Your assignment is to assume the role of historian and fill in the facts that are missing from the passage below. Use classroom and library resources to help you figure out which words go in the blanks.

During the_____1. dynasty, which ruled from 206 B.C. to A.D. 220, China's military

power and cultural influence increased greatly. In the first century B.C._____

2. was introduced from_____3. It became a major religion of China. A merchant from

Italy named_____4. went to China in 1275, and stayed 20 years. After overthrow-

ing the Mongols, the_____5. Dynasty began in 1368. China's capital was moved from

Nanjing to_____6. in 1421. In 1644 the_____7. conquered China

and set up the_____8. dynasty. In the nineteenth century Japan and a

few_____9. countries gained control of China's trade. China became a republic under

Dr._____10. in 1912. Following World War II, in 1949, the_____11. Party

took over China. The leader of the Communists was_____12. In the 1950s

the United States fought against China in the_____13. War. In 1959 an uprising

by_____14. in western China was crushed with Chinese troops. Diplomatic rela-

tions between China and the United States were established in_____15. In

1989 Chinese troops smashed pro-democracy protests held at_____16. Square.

Name _____

Graphing China's Population

China's current population is around 1.2 billion, and it is projected to reach over 1.3 billion by the year 2000. Although China's economy is growing, overpopulation helps keep the nation poor. Listed below are population figures for China for selected years. Use the figures to construct a bar graph. After you have completed the graph, answer the questions below.

Year	Population
2140 B.C.	13,500,000
771 B.C.	20,000,000
A.D. 220	60,000,000
752	80,000,000
1840	413,000,000
1949	542,000,000
1960	662,000,000
1970	830,000,000
1980	1,015,000,000
1993	1,200,000,000

1. Describe China's population between 2140 B.C. and A.D. 1993. _____

2. What are some possible reasons for China's population increases? _____

_____

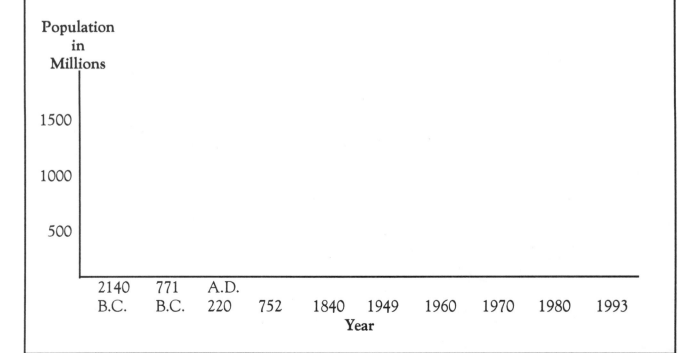

Japan

Far across the Pacific Ocean is a place that has surmounted enormous difficulties to become one of the most prosperous countries in the world. This is Japan, an island nation about the size of California, which, after World War II, lay in ruins and defeat and which has few natural resources to support economic growth. The key to Japan's prosperity is international trade. Today, Japan has transformed itself into a top industrial nation known throughout the world for the quality of its high-tech products, such as cars, electronics, and computers. Although a modern nation, Japan has a rich cultural heritage. Some Japanese festivals have been celebrated for over 1,400 years, and Japan's ancient capital, Kyoto, has a 1,200-year history. Along with traditional temples, shrines, gardens, bridges, and other human-made treasures, the Japanese are careful to preserve their country's natural beauty. Even with a population of around 125 million and numerous large cities, the Japanese are never far from mountains, forests, rivers, or the sea.

Mount Fuji is Japan's highest peak and national symbol. On which island is it located?

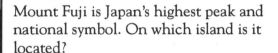

INVESTIGATIONS

What is the name of the traditional Japanese garment worn by both men and women?

This wooden gateway, or *torii*, found at the entrance to shrines throughout Japan, is the symbol of the nation's oldest surviving religion. What is the religion's name?

Language Arts: The Japanese language is written using a combination of Chinese pictorial characters called *kanji* and modified Chinese characters which denote syllables called *kana.* Japanese students spend considerable time in school studying calligraphy, which is the practice of using a finely-pointed ink brush to make the hundreds of Japanese characters correctly and artfully. Let students try their hands at calligraphy. Give them the characters below, which mean "Japan," to copy.

Art: Japanese wood block print art is world famous. For centuries, Japanese artists have created prints of scenes from everyday life. The steps in making a Japanese print are as follows. First, artists draw the scene on a block of wood. Then, they carve away the wood which is not part of the drawing, leaving the raised drawing. Next, they apply one color of paint to the raised surface. Finally, a piece of paper is pressed against the surface to create the print. Students will enjoy practicing the printing techniques of Japanese artisans. But before students start, give them a variety of examples of Japanese print art (illustrations of Japanese print art can be found in art books from the school or community library), and let them practice sketching their drawings on scratch paper until they are satisfied with them. (You may also want to provide students with some Japanese scenes on transparencies projected on the wall for them to trace). To make the prints, provide students with 1/4" to 1/2" thick pieces of porous, easy-to-cut Styrofoam, which will substitute for the wood blocks, and dull plastic knives, which can be used to carve the Styrofoam pieces. (Additional safe objects for carving can be used at your discretion.) They will also need absorbent paper and water-based powder paints in an assortment of colors.

History: The history of Japan is rich and long. Have students use library resources to report on the following aspects of Japanese history: Tokugawa period, Meiji period, Russo-Japanese War, World War II, period of Allied military occupation, and Japan today.

Literature: Check the school and community libraries for books about Japan by both American and Japanese writers. Let students listen to you read some Japanese poems, called *haiku.* Although brief, haiku poems convey powerful ideas and feelings, and they provide insights into Japanese values and traditions. Some students might want to read *The Big Wave,* a popular story about Japan written by American author Pearl Buck.

Sports: Let interested students report to the class on sumo wrestling, which is a very popular spectator sport in Japan.

Japanese Festivals

Like people everywhere, the Japanese have special occasions which they celebrate year after year. Some Japanese celebrations are local. For example, at Nakaniida, a town in northeastern Japan, children put on handmade tiger costumes to perform a tiger dance to the musical accompaniment of flutes and drums. The Tiger Dance Festival is based upon an ancient myth that a tiger commands the winds. Since for centuries a strong seasonal wind has whipped up dangerous fires around Nakaniida, the tiger dance was a way to please the tiger god and prevent fires. The Tiger Dance Festival is now a 300-year-old tradition.

A national festival which is celebrated in both the United States and Japan is New Year's Day. After reading the description of Japan's New Year festivities, respond to the following directions on a separate sheet of paper: (1) research and then describe the history of New Year's Day celebrations in the United States, (2) interview some other students about how they and their families celebrate New Year's Day, (3) compare and contrast the New Year's Day festivities for Japan and the United States, and (4) describe a local festival which has become a tradition in your community.

New Year is Japan's biggest holiday. The Japanese celebrate the New Year for three days, January first through third. Families decorate the front entrances of their houses with *kado-matsu*, which is usually a pair of pine trees, which denote long life. Behind the pine trees are placed three stems of bamboo, which represent constancy and virtue. Another decoration at the entrance to the house is the *shimenawa*, or taboo-rope. On this rope are hung tufts of straw and strips of white paper. To these decorations are added fern leaves, an orange, and a small lobster, which symbolize good wishes for a long, prosperous life.

On the first day of the holiday the whole family dresses in their best clothes for a trip to the local shrine. Families also exchange visits with friends and relatives. On the second day are ceremonies related to beginning all sorts of activities in the hope that by starting the activities on this special occasion the participants will do them well throughout the year. For example, young children might begin the study of calligraphy, or writing the Japanese language, on this day. Traditionally, during this festival boys fly kites and girls play badminton. The favorite indoor games of the season are a card game known as *irohagaruta* and a backgammon game called *sugoroku*.

Japan's Urban Centers

Imagine cramming about half of the total population of the whole United States into California, then you can get some idea of what it would be like to live in one of the world's more densely packed places–Japan. The Tokyo Bay area of Japan (1,089 square miles), which includes Japan's capital, Tokyo, and the port city of Yokohama, contains over 18 million people, making it one of the largest metropolitan areas in the world. While the Tokyo Bay area is the most extreme case, living space–and its scarcity–is a big problem in urban areas throughout Japan. Below are an outline map of Japan and a list of some of Japan's largest cities. Use a map of Japan in an encyclopedia or atlas to find the cities, plot their locations, and label them on the map below. What do the locations of the cities tell you about population centers in Japan?

_____

_____

Chiba   Fukuoka
Hiroshima   Kawasaki
Kitakyushu   Kobe
Kyoto   Nagoya
Osaka   Sapporo
Tokyo   Yokohama

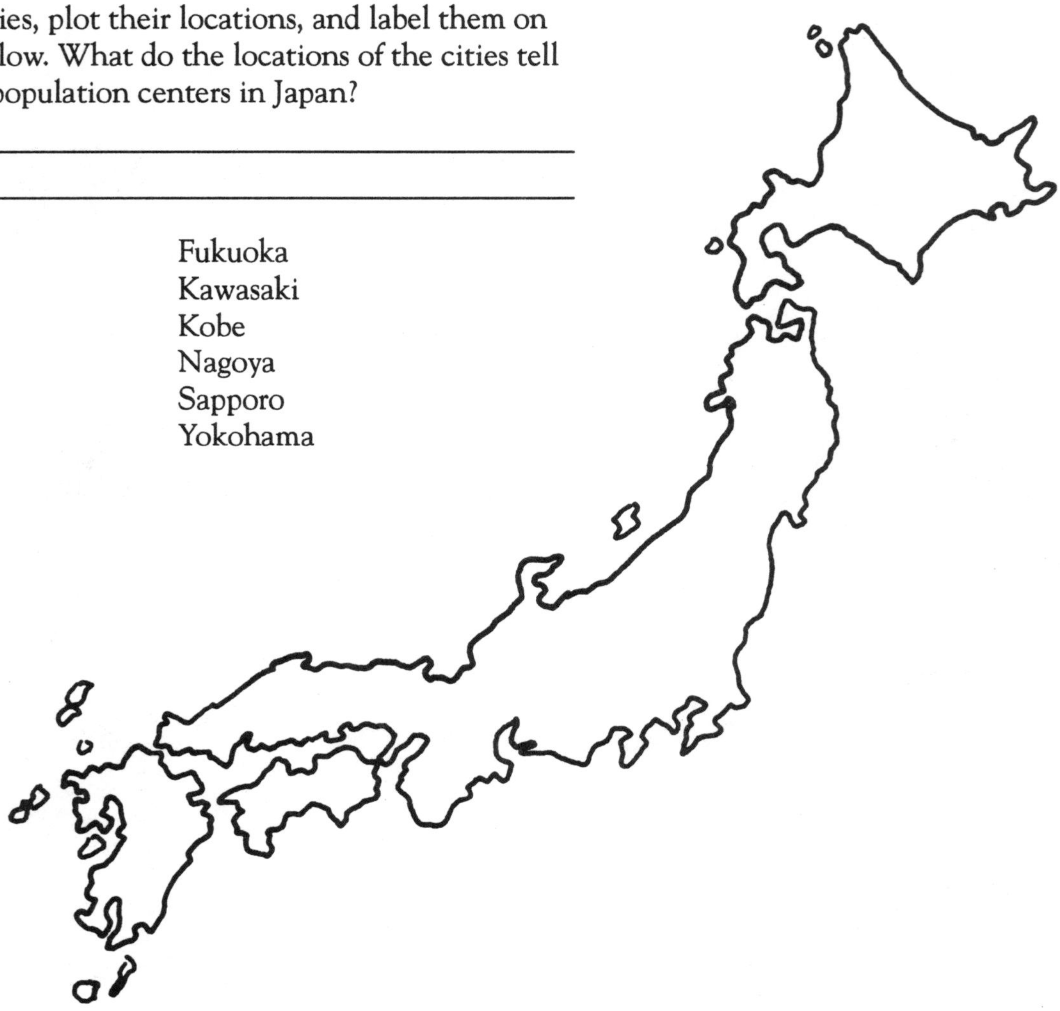

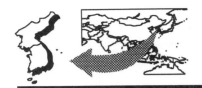

Korea

Viewed from space, the Korean peninsula, separated from the rest of Asia by sea and mountains, looks like an isolated and peaceful place. However, frequent invasions by China and Japan, the occupation of North Korea by the Soviet Union after World War II, and North Korea's invasion of South Korea and the ensuing Korean War have been a big part of Korea's often turbulent history. Despite centuries under the domination of powerful neighbors, Koreans have managed to maintain their cultural identity. In the southern part of the peninsula, the Republic of Korea's free market economy has emerged in the 1990s as one of Asia's biggest success stories. South Korea's major exports include textiles and clothing, electrical machinery, shoes, steel, and cars. Seoul, the capital of South Korea, is a modern, industrial city of around 11 million people. In comparison, Communist-led North Korea, despite an abundance of natural resources, has experienced almost none of the South Korea's prosperity.

This huge Dragon Drum was part of the Summer Olympic ceremonies held in Seoul. When were the Seoul Olympics held?

This is one of Korea's traditional musical instruments. What is it called?

INVESTIGATIONS

Early sculptures in Korea of this image reflect the influence of a major religion brought from China. What is the name of the religion?

History: To introduce the study of Korea, provide students with the following historical overview but with the italicized words deleted. Let students use library resources and context clues to identify the missing words. Korea first became a *unified* country in A.D. 668 when it came under *Shilla* rule. Throughout most of Korea's history, the nation tended to have long-term and stable governments. The last dynasty, called the *Yi* dynasty or Choson Kingdom, lasted 500 years, as did the one previous to it, the *Koryo* dynasty. In the late sixteenth century *Japanese* invasions brought devastation to Korea. The Japanese invasions strongly influenced Korea's deliberate policy of *isolationism*, which was to last *250* years and which helped earn the nation the title of "The Hermit Kingdom." During the last half of the *nineteenth* century, foreign meddling in *Korean* affairs brought the period of isolationism to an end. Japan gained a strong foothold on the peninsula, and in 1910 *Korea* became a colony of Japan. In the 1930s Japanese treatment of Koreans was especially harsh. For example, the Japanese took *rice* which was needed to feed hungry Koreans and *exported* it to Japan. They also forced Koreans to give up their Korean names and take *Japanese*-style names. In 1948 the Republic of *Korea* was established with Syngman *Rhee* as its first president. Shortly thereafter, communist-controlled *North* Korea was established. In 1950 the *Korean War* broke out when North Korean troops stormed across the *thirty-eighth* parallel into South Korea. An armistice was signed in *1953*. It established a demilitarized zone (DMZ) between the two Koreas. South Korea has three major goals for the future. They are to maintain the country's booming *economy*, move from authoritarianism toward *democracy*, and explore ways to *unify* the two Koreas.

Critical Thinking: Have students compare the symbols found on the South Korean and North Korean flags and coat of arms. Based upon their analysis, what can students infer about the two Korean societies? (South Korea's symbols represent ancient, universal Oriental beliefs, while North Korea's symbols represent communism and practical economic matters.)

Culture: Ask a Korean-American person from the community to share information about his/her cultural heritage with the class.

Geography: Have students draw maps of Korea which include the following geographic features: major mountains, rivers, cities, and bodies of water.

Current Events: Students can survey their homes and other students to develop a list of Korean-made products that are sold and used in the United States. Have students examine newspapers and news magazines for articles about Korea. They can bring them to class to share with other students.

Korea's Cultural Heritage

Unlike most East Asian countries, the Republic of Korea does not adhere to any one religious mainstream. Instead, the nation has been open to a broad spectrum of religious beliefs. Use library resources to investigate the religions on the right, which are an important part of Korean culture. Then match the religions with characteristics or events associated with them on the left. Put the correct letter on the blank space.

Characteristic   **Religion**

____ 1. The folk worship of many different forces in nature

____ 2. Brought to Korea by Indian and Tibetan monks

____ 3. Places a strong emphasis on social ethics

____ 4. Eight million Koreans are members

____ 5. Associated with modernism

____ 6. Loyalty to friends and ancestor worship are important virtues

____ 7. At one time was the state religion

____ 8. The most popular symbol is a crane

____ 9 Teachings were a basis for government and administration

____ 10. The first missionary came with a Japanese invasion force

____ 11. The decline in its influence can be traced to an invasion of the Mongols

A. Shamanism

B. Buddhism

C   Confucianism

D. Christianity

Comparing South and North Korea

After World War II, the Korean peninsula was divided into two zones, north and south of 38°
north latitude. The two zones later evolved into two countries: the Democratic People's Republic
of Korea, or North Korea, and the Republic of Korea, or South Korea. Use library resources to
compare and contrast the two Koreas. Use the retrieval chart below to organize your analysis.

		South Korea	North Korea
1.	Land area		
2.	Major cities		
3.	Population		
4.	Ethnic groups		
6.	Religion(s)		
7.	Government		
8.	Head of government		
9.	Foreign policy		
10.	Per capita GNP (Gross National Product)		
11.	Chief crops		
12.	Natural resources		
13.	Major industries		
14.	Chief exports		

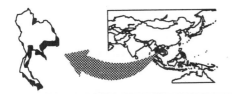

Thailand

Thailand is a kaleidoscopic blend of old and new. The country's respect for its heritage is epitomized in traditional Thai products, customs, and monuments. Thai silk, gems, and jewelry are world famous for their quality and beauty. Gorgeously costumed classical dancers and saffron-robed Buddhist monks are timeless examples of Thai cultural traditions. Stunning Thai temples, such as Wat Arun, and the ruins of ancient kingdoms, like Ayutthaya, are among the many architectural treasures. With its high-rise office buildings and hotels, Thailand's involvement with modern progress is apparent in the capital city of Bangkok. Called *Krung Thep*, or "City of Angels," by the Thai people, Bangkok is the nation's industrial, commercial, and financial center. Today, Thailand has one of Asia's fastest growing economies. Thailand's unique blend of the traditional and modern has also made the country one of Asia's most popular tourist destinations.

INVESTIGATIONS

The main focus of Thailand's farmers is on growing this important crop. Name the crop.

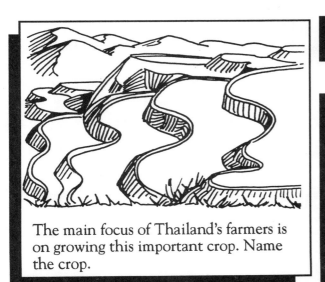

Magnificent temples are found throughout Thailand, revealing the influence of the country's major religion. What is the name of the religion?

One of Thailand's famous floating markets is found in the nation's capital city. What is the capital's name?

Curriculum Connections

Food and Diet: Thai food is growing in popularity around the world. Although influenced by the cooking of China, India, Indonesia, Malaysia, and Portugal, Thai food has its own special tastes and aromas. Rice is served at most Thai meals, along with a curry dish, fish, and yam. Vegetables are usually stir-fried. The ingredients for a Thai curry include coconut milk, lemon grass, shrimp paste, fish sauce, and chili peppers. Thais eat their food with a fork and large spoon. Have students select a food from Thailand to investigate. Easy-to-prepare Thai soup and sauce mixes are available at many supermarkets. The Thais often eat fresh fruit for dessert. You might want to share one or more of these favorite Thai fruits with your students: mangoes, bananas, coconut, papaya, pineapple, guava, and lychees.

Economy: Although Thailand has modern industries and manufacturing plants, the basis of the Thai economy and the main occupation of Thai farmers is the production of rice. To ensure a good rice harvest, a special ritual, called the Royal Plowing Ceremony, is held in Bangkok at the beginning of the rice season in May. At the ceremony, rice seeds are scattered and predictions are made about the forthcoming harvest. Rice farming in Thailand is a cooperative enterprise. Using water buffalo to plow the fields, all of the villagers work together to make certain the fields are ready for planting by the time the first rains come. Everyone also participates in planting the rice seedlings by hand. By November, when the rice is ready to harvest, groups of villagers cut the rice by hand and spread it in the fields to dry. From there it is taken to the family compounds for threshing and winnowing, which is usually completed by January. Have students investigate the steps in rice farming in Thailand. Based on what they learn about the process, ask them to share insights they have gained about country life in Thailand.

Sports: Some students might want to research traditional Thai-style boxing. This sport, which is also a means of self-defense, allows the boxers to use their feet as well as their hands. One sport students might want to try is Takro, which is played with a woven rattan ball. The objective of the sport is to keep the ball in the air by using almost every part of the body but the hands.

Geography/Mathematics: Bangkok's Don Muang International Airport is served by almost 50 airlines from around the world. Have students use globes and string to calculate the miles from Bangkok to the following cities flying nonstop: Sydney, Australia; Calcutta, India; Jakarta, Indonesia; Honolulu, Hawaii; and Paris, France.

Buddhism in Thailand

You are never very far away from Buddhism in Thailand. Almost everywhere you look there is a Buddhist temple—there are over 400 in Bangkok alone! And it is very likely that you will meet a group of Buddhist monks, dressed in their bright saffron-colored robes, as they make their morning rounds for alms or gifts of food. To find out more about Buddhism, use library resources to answer the following questions.

1. When, where, and by whom was Buddhism founded?

   _____

   _____

   _____

2. Why was Buddhism founded? The basic teachings of Buddhism include the Noble Eightfold Path. What are the eight elements of the path? Do you think the eight elements are noble?

   _____

   _____

   _____

3. Buddhist monks are expected to follow certain rules which guide their lives. What rules must they follow?

   _____

   _____

   _____

4. Meditation is one of the most popular aspects of Buddhism. What are the fundamentals of meditation?

   _____

   _____

   _____

   _____

   _____

   _____

Name _____

Colorful Thailand

Imagine you are on a four-day vacation in Thailand. Each day you visit attractions of interest. You record your thoughts and recollections of each day's events in a notebook, which will be shared with a special friend when you return home. The notebook entries for each day of the trip have been started for you below. Your task is to finish the entries. Before you begin writing, use your research skills to investigate each of the topics so that your entries about Thailand will be as accurate as possible. Be certain to use colorful adjectives to describe the things that happened on the trip.

Day 1: The Buddhist temples in Thailand are gorgeous. Among the most splendid is Wat Phra Kaeo. The wondrous temple decoration includes . . .

_____
_____
_____

Day 2: Unlike most Southeast Asian countries, Thailand has never been a European colony. Today, the guide told us about Thailand's early history. She said . . .

_____
_____
_____

Day 3: There are so many things to see and do in Bangkok. Some of my favorite attractions were . . .

_____
_____
_____

Day 4: Today we had a chance to go shopping. Some of the traditional Thai products I especially liked were . . .

_____
_____
_____

Indonesia

Indonesia is the world's largest island nation. Indonesia's over 17,000 islands span some 3,200 miles between the Asian mainland and Australia. Indonesia's land area is almost three times the size of Texas, and with about 193 million people, it is the fourth most populous nation in the world. Columbus discovered America while looking for the Indies, which was what Indonesia was then called. In the sixteenth century the Dutch arrived. They gained control of the spice trade and dominated the area for 350 years. Indonesia's people are very diverse culturally; they are comprised of Malays, Javanese, Bataks, Balinese, Chinese, Dayaks, and over 300 other ethnic groups. Tropical rain forests, which still cover 75 percent of the land, are the habitat of a tremendous variety of animals, including endangered Sumatran rhinos, orangutans, tigers, and elephants. Indonesia declared its independence from the Netherlands in 1945, but it took four years of fighting to push out the Dutch. Indonesia's economy is growing. Besides traditional exports of spices, rubber, and palm oil, the island nation is the largest oil exporter in Southeast Asia, as well as the world's largest exporter of liquefied natural gas and plywood.

Indonesia's most famous volcano killed more than 35,000 people on Java when it erupted in 1883. What was the name of the volcano?

INVESTIGATIONS

The world's largest lizard, which may grow to six feet in length, is found only on a few small islands in Indonesia. What is the lizard called?

What is the mythical bird called that is displayed on Indonesia's coat of arms?

Drama: In Indonesia ancient stories are transmitted from one generation to the next through a performance called *wayang kulit purwo,* or "leather puppets shadow play." To create the performance, a light is directed at the flat leather puppets to cast a shadow against a screen which is viewed by the audience. With musical accompaniment, the puppeteer manipulates and speaks for the puppets to make the shadows come alive. Most of the stories for the wayang, or play, are drawn from ancient Hindu epics, and they are designed to convey moral and ethical teachings. For example, one epic, called *Ramayana,* is about the role of "good," played by Rama and Sinta, as it is pitted against the role of "evil," played by Rahwana, a 10-headed giant. The leather puppets, like the one illustrated here, are elaborately designed and crafted. Students can make their own Indonesian shadow puppets and perform their own plays by following these simple steps.

1. Sketch the outline of the puppet on a piece of heavy construction paper. (Make the puppet about 1 to 1½-foot high).

2. Cut out the puppet. Cut the lower and upper arms in two separate pieces.

3. Use fold-back pins to attach the arm pieces at the shoulders and elbows.

4. Attach one end of a two-foot-long stick to each of the puppet's hands. (The sticks are used to move the puppet.)

Science: Indonesia is a land of more than 200 volcanic mountains, of which around 100 are active. The country is located on the "Ring of Fire," which is the description given to a line of active volcanoes that dot the Pacific. In the past, volcanic activity in Indonesia has been deadly. The eruption of Mt. Krakatau in 1883 killed more than 35,000 people. Have students research this famous eruption as well as other eruptions which have occurred in Indonesia. Interested students can also investigate the "Ring of Fire" and should illustrate their reports with maps and diagrams.

Art: Indonesians make beautifully decorated cloth called *batik.* The batik designs are made by waxing and dyeing the cloth. After a design is drawn on the cloth, wax is used to cover areas which are not to be colored when the cloth is dipped in the dye. The process is repeated with different colors, and each time wax is used to cover the newly dyed areas. With the help of your art teacher, you might want to let your students try their hand at making Indonesian-style batik cloth.

Exotic Indonesia

Listed below are some of the world's most rare and exotic plants and animals, all of which can be found in Indonesia. Use library resources to research them. Then describe each one briefly in the space provided.

1. One-Horned Rhinoceros: _____

_____

2. Asian Elephant: _____

_____

3. Babirusa: _____

_____

4. Bali Mynah: _____

_____

5. Orangutan: _____

_____

6. Komodo Dragon: _____

_____

7. Anoa: _____

_____

8. Bird of Paradise: _____

_____

9. Rafflesia: _____

_____

10. Durian: _____

_____

11. Cassowary: _____

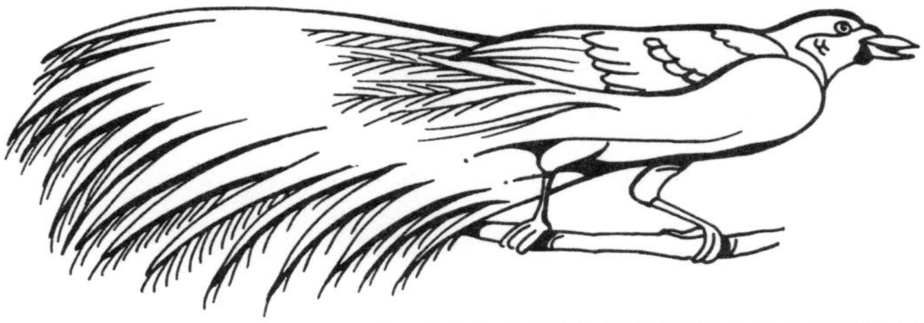

_____

Indonesian Island Hopping

With over 17,000 islands, Indonesia is an island hoppers paradise. On the right are listed some of Indonesia's major islands. Use library resources to research the islands. Then match the islands with their characteristics, which are listed on the left. Put the correct letter on the blank.

Characteristic

_____ 1. Has over 60 percent of Indonesia's population

_____ 2. Home of the Dayak people

_____ 3. Part of New Guinea

_____ 4. Location of Indonesia's capital city

_____ 5. Location of Lake Toba, Asia's largest fresh water lake

_____ 6. Indonesia's largest national park is found here

_____ 7. The people on this island are mostly Hindu

_____ 8. Home of the Batak people

_____ 9. Location of Indonesia's highest mountain

_____ 10. Indonesia's most mountainous island

_____ 11. The sixth largest island in the world

_____ 12. Known as the *Spice Islands*

_____ 13. Westernmost island of Indonesia

_____ 14. About the same size as France

_____ 15. Part of Melanesia

_____ 16. Location of the world's largest Buddhist monument

Island

A. Bali

B. Sumatra

C. Java

D. Moluccas

E. Kalimantan

F. Sulawesi

G. Irian Jaya

The Pacific World

An Overview for the Teacher

The Pacific Ocean extends from the Arctic Circle to Antarctica and from the Americas to Australia. This vast area covers some 70 million square miles and surrounds more than 25,000 islands. Both the "island continent" of Australia and the island nation of New Zealand are part of the Pacific World. Make a transparency of the outline map of the Pacific World on the next page. Ask students to identify Australia, New Zealand, and the various island countries and cultures of Micronesia, Melanesia, and Polynesia.

Historically, Australia and New Zealand were part of the British Empire. Colonial Australia and New Zealand were connected culturally, politically, and economically to Britain but isolated from the rest of the world. In the 1890s it took the fastest steamship 16 days to carry mail across the Pacific Ocean and the fastest sailing ship 35 days to carry cargo from San Francisco to Sydney, Australia. The United States' interest in the Pacific World was heightened by the acquisition of California and Oregon in the 1840s. Hawaii was visited by American whalers and missionaries, and the city of Honolulu became an important American outpost and naval station. Before the Spanish-American War, few Americans had ever heard of the Philippines or Guam. But after 1898, the acquisition of those Spanish possessions, along with the annexation of Hawaii, made the United States a major power in the Pacific. During World War II, because of the intense and bloody fighting in the Solomons, Gilberts, Marshalls, and Marianas, placenames in the Pacific World became American household words. After World War II, the United States was given responsibility by the United Nations to administer the U.S. Trust Territory of the Pacific Islands (Micronesia). Today, the United States still has a number of territories and possessions in the Pacific World including American Samoa, Guam, Midway Islands, Northern Mariana Islands, Trust Territory of the Pacific Islands (Palau), and Wake Island. Australia, France, New Zealand, and Britain also have territories in the Pacific. Independent Pacific island nations include Western Samoa, Vanuatu, Tuvalu, Tonga, Solomon Islands, Papua New Guinea, Nauru, Micronesia, Marshall Islands, Kiribati, and Fiji.

Today, high technology, jet travel, and international trade have brought the nations of the Pacific World closer together. Australia's and New Zealand's traditional links with Britain and Europe are being replaced by new trade relationships with countries along the Pacific rim, including Japan, South Korea, China, and the United States. John Maxwell Hamilton, in his book *Entangling Alliances*, shows how flexibility, speed, and the global work force have made geographic proximity almost irrelevant. He tells about a New Zealander who, after working for IBM in New Zealand, started his own data entry services company in Sydney, Australia, subcontracted the work in Singapore, and later opened offices in the Philippines and the United States. Increasingly, technological advances are bringing countries of the world closer together.

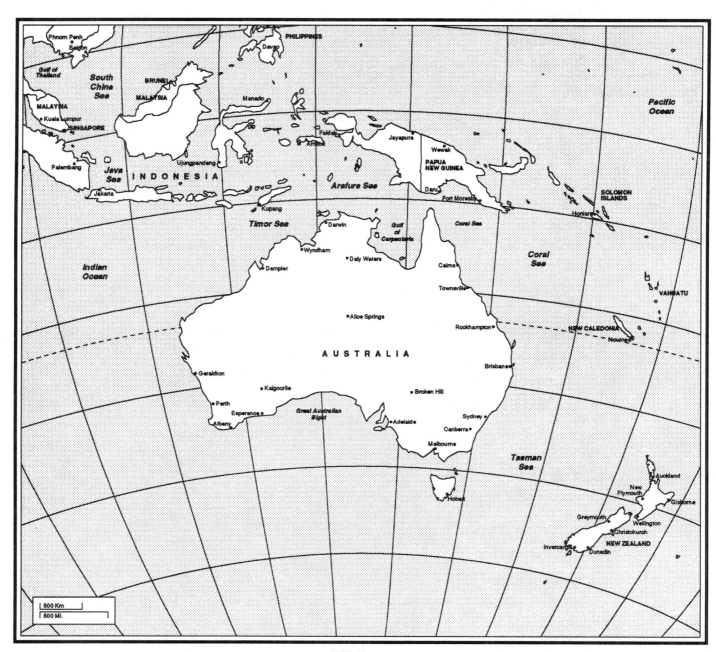

The
Pacific World

62   FS-10124 Countries and Cultures

Australia

Australia is both a continent and a country. It is the world's driest and flattest continent and the world's sixth largest nation in land area. Despite its huge size, Australia's population is only about 17 million, which is just 2.5 million more than New York City's urban area. Because of Australia's geographic isolation, the country has a unique assortment of plants and animals, with strange sounding names like kookaburra and wombat, not found elsewhere on earth. Although most of Australia's original inhabitants, the aborigines, live in cities and towns, some still remain in the remote "outback" and hold on to their rich traditions. Among the first Europeans to settle in Australia in the late eighteenth century were convicts from Britain. Later, free settlers came to farm the land or mine the goldfields. Today, most Australians live in large coastal cities like Sydney, Melbourne, Brisbane, and Adelaide, located in the southeastern part of the country. The Australian people enjoy a high standard of living. They also love sports. Among the most popular sports are rugby, tennis, swimming, fishing, cricket, bush walking, boating, and riding horses.

The Australian flag is the only one to fly over a whole continent. What do the stars on the flag signify?

INVESTIGATIONS

The Koala bear is native to Australia. What is the main food in the diet of the Koala?

This building is considered one of the architectural and engineering achievements of the twentieth century. What is the building called?

Economics: Australia has the fifteenth largest economy in the world. The nation leads the world in wool production. In fact, Australia has nine sheep for every one person! Among the chief crops produced are wheat, barley, and sugar. Australia is one of the world's main producers of minerals and metals. The country has major deposits of quartzite, coal, sand, gold, lead, zinc, iron, copper, nickel, manganese, uranium, and diamonds. After Japan, the United States is Australia's biggest trading partner. Have students research Australia's economy. They can report on the following areas: tourism, agriculture, manufacturing, services, and industries.

Language Arts: Australia's vast landscape, untamed wilderness, and rugged beauty have inspired writers and poets. It has been called a "fantastic land of monstrosities," described as "full of surprises, and adventures, and incongruities, and incredibilities" and "a sunburnt country" of "beauty" and "terror." Show students pictures that reflect Australia's climatic and geographical diversity. Then ask students to react to the scenes by writing down words or phrases that convey their feelings and thoughts. After they have finished, ask volunteers to share their reactions with the class.

Science: Australia's Great Barrier Reef is the world's largest coral reef. It extends 1,250 miles along Australia's northeastern coast and incorporates 2,900 individual coral reefs and some 1,500 species of fish. Have students research the Great Barrier Reef. They can report on the reef's formation and geography, the species of corals and fish found there, and the ecology and conservation of the reef system.

Culture: It is thought that Australia's aborigines came to Australia some 40,000 years ago from Southeast Asia. The nomadic aborigines roamed the land hunting, fishing, and gathering food. They traveled light and carried only a few essential items: a boomerang, a wooden spear with a barbed point, a *woomera* or spearthrowing device, a hitting stick called a *nullanulla*, a shield, a stone knife, an axe, a small collection of wooden bowls, and sticks to start fires. When Europeans arrived in Australia, the aborigines were scattered over most of the land and spoke many languages and dialects. Today, only a few aborigines still follow a nomadic way of life. One of the most interesting aspects of aboriginal traditional culture is their belief in the *Dreamtime*. Dreamtime was when huge creatures, called *Bunyips*, awoke from their sleep and wandered across the earth. As they walked, looking for food and water, their great size created rivers, valleys, and all of the world's other features. According to tradition, aboriginal life was created during the Dreamtime, and at that time their ancestors were taught how they should behave and care for the land. Encourage students to find out more about aboriginal tools, beliefs, traditions, and art.

Speaking Australian

Although English is spoken in Australia, some Australian words might sound strange to American ears. See if you can correctly match the Australian words and phrases on the left with their American equivalent on the right. Put the correct letter in the blank space.

Australian

_____ 1. G'day

_____ 2. Mate

_____ 3. Lollies

_____ 4. Fair dinkum

_____ 5. Aussie

_____ 6. Bloke

_____ 7. Ta

_____ 8. Crook

_____ 9. Brolly

_____ 10. Biscuits

_____ 11. Lorry

_____ 12. Petrol

_____ 13. Pictures

_____ 14. Bush

_____ 15. Lounge

_____ 16. Sandshoes

_____ 17. Station

_____ 18. Footpath

_____ 19. Chips

_____ 20. Barbie

_____ 21. Digger

_____ 22. Cozzie

American

A. Sick

B. Umbrella

C. Large ranch

D. Movies

E. Bathing suit

F. Sidewalk

G. French fries

H. Gas

I. Sneakers

J. Cookout

K. Candy

L. Friend

M. Australian

N. Thank you

O. Man

P. Genuine, honest

Q. Hello

R. Living room

S. Truck

T. Country

U. Cookies

V. Soldier

Amazing Australia

Australia has more unique animals than any other area in the world. On the left are listed some animals that are native only to Australia. Match the Australian animals with their correct descriptions on the right. Put the correct letter in the blank space.

Australian Animal

_____ 1. Echidna

_____ 2. Platypus

_____ 3. Wallabies

_____ 4. Tasmanian devil

_____ 5. Bandicoot

_____ 6. Wombat

_____ 7. Numbat

_____ 8. Dingo

_____ 9. Emu

_____ 10. Kookaburra

_____ 11. Lyrebird

_____ 12. Budgerigars

_____ 13. Boobook

_____ 14. Brolga

_____ 15. Goannas

_____ 16. Taipan

_____ 17. Frilled lizard

_____ 18. Kangaroo

_____ 19. Koala

_____ 20. Galahs

Description

A. Largest bird in Australia

B. Giant kingfisher

C. Poisonous snake

D. Peacock-like bird

E. Squirrel-like anteater

F. Australia's best known marsupial

G. Tree-dwelling, bear-like

H. Wild dog

I. Small kangaroos

J. Black fur, powerful jaws

K. Lovebirds

L. Badger-like

M. Colorful parrots

N. "Rat-pig"

O. Spiny anteater

P. Awful looking when angry

Q. Crane

R. Type of monitor lizards

S. Rubbery bill, webbed feet

T. Owl

New Zealand

New Zealand was settled more than a thousand years ago by the Maori people, who came from Polynesia. In 1642 the Dutch became the first Europeans to visit the islands. New Zealand was claimed for Britain by Captain James Cook in 1769. The 1840 Treaty of Waitangi between the British Crown and Maori chiefs gave the British the right to settle in New Zealand and promised to protect Maori land. But the promise was not kept, and after many years of fighting, much of the Maori's land was seized. Today, the Maori people make up about 12 percent of New Zealand's total population of 3.5 million. New Zealand consists of two main islands. There is North Island, where two-thirds of the people live and where the capital, Wellington, is located, and there is South Island, which is the site of some of the world's most spectacular mountains and glaciers. Although most New Zealanders live in cities and towns, agriculture is the country's number one industry. Sheep outnumber people in New Zealand by 20 to 1, which gives some idea of how important this one animal is to the nation's economy.

INVESTIGATIONS

What is the name of this tailless and flightless bird that is only found in New Zealand?

New Zealand's tallest mountain, which was named for a famous British sea captain, is 12,349 feet high. What is it called?

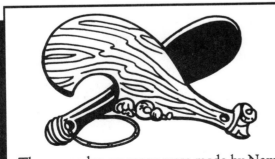

These wooden weapons were made by New Zealand's traditional inhabitants. Who are they?

Curriculum Connections

Culture: The Maori people are one of many Polynesian groups who traveled thousands of miles in outrigger canoes in search of a new home. Many islands located throughout the South Pacific were settled by Polynesians. Let interested students research the early history of the Maori people. They can report on various aspects of their culture, including their language, beliefs, economic system, food sources, family life, and social organization. They can also investigate other Polynesian island groups in the South Pacific, such as those found on Fiji, Tonga, Nauru, Samoa, and Tahiti.

Science: About three-quarters of New Zealand's electricity needs are met by hydrogeneration. Geothermal power is also used to generate electricity. Have students describe the physical geography of New Zealand that relates to these two important sources of electrical power.

Mathematics: Like most of the world's countries, New Zealand uses the metric system. Have students calculate the distances in both miles and kilometers between Auckland, New Zealand, and Hong Kong, London, Los Angeles, New York, Sydney, and Tokyo. Below are some possible answers. Accept any reasonable answers.

	Kilometers	Miles
Hong Kong	11,307	7,023
London	22,865	14,202
Los Angeles	12,852	7,983
New York	17,275	10,730
Sydney	2,162	1,343
Tokyo	13,583	8,437

Language Arts: Show students pictures that reflect the diversity and beauty of New Zealand's geography. Then have them use metaphors and similes to describe the scenery. For example, New Zealand's lakes might be described as "clear as crystal" or an "azure mirror," or its beaches might be described as a "long white cloud" or "white as snow."

Government: New Zealand is an independent democratic nation. As a member of the British Commonwealth of Nations, New Zealand has an executive branch of government, which is headed by a Governor General appointed by the British Monarch. Real power, however, is held by the legislative branch, or Parliament. Parliament consists of a single-chamber House of Representatives. The 97 members of Parliament are elected by the voters. The leader of the majority political party in Parliament is the head of the government. The leader's title is Prime Minister. Have students research New Zealand's government. How does it compare to the United States' system of government?

Climate: Since New Zealand's seasons are reversed, students might want to compare the following maximum temperatures for Auckland, New Zealand with those of their own community: December–February, 23° C; June–August, 15° C.

Made in New Zealand

What can New Zealand's products tell you about the country and its people? The information below shows the main products that New Zealand exports or sells to other countries. Also listed are New Zealand's main export markets ("markets" mean the countries that buy New Zealand's products). Values for exports are in New Zealand dollars (NZ$). One U.S. dollar equals NZ$1.60. Use the information to answer the questions below.

Main Export Products	NZ$ million	Main Export Markets	NZ$ million
Meat	2,422.	Japan	2,655.
Wool	1,795.	Australia	2,424.
Forest products	1,172.	United States	1,912.
Aluminum	875.	Britain	1,008.
Fruit and vegetables	824.	China	538.
Hides, skins, and fur	725.	South Korea	468.
Butter	609.		
Fish	537.		

What is life like in New Zealand? The lists of New Zealand's main export products and markets might help you answer this question. Do the products tell you anything about occupations and industries in New Zealand? Do the products and export markets tell you anything about the history and geography of New Zealand?

1. List some of the occupations that you think might be important in New Zealand.

_____

_____

2. List some of the industries that you think might be important in New Zealand.

_____

_____

3. List some of the geographic features that you think might be found in New Zealand.

_____

_____

New Zealand Cartography

New Zealand lies in the South Pacific Ocean midway between the equator and the South Pole. It is about the same size as Britain or Colorado. Use library resources to identify the New Zealand geographic features described below and to find their locations on a map. Then plot the locations on the outline map below. Use the blank spaces for the answers and use the numbers corresponding to the features to indicate their locations on the map.

1. World's biggest crater lake
   _____

2. Longest river
   _____

3. Capital
   _____

4. Sea off west coast
   _____

5. Place where 1840 treaty was
   signed _____

6. Highest mountain
   _____

7. Name of third largest island
   _____

8. Volcanic plateau is in center of
   this island_____

9. This island has glaciers and 15
   peaks over 10,000 feet._____
   _____

10. Third largest city
    _____

11. Water passage between the two
    main islands _____

12. Name of mountain range at
    44° south latitude and 77° east
    longitude _____

13. Largest city

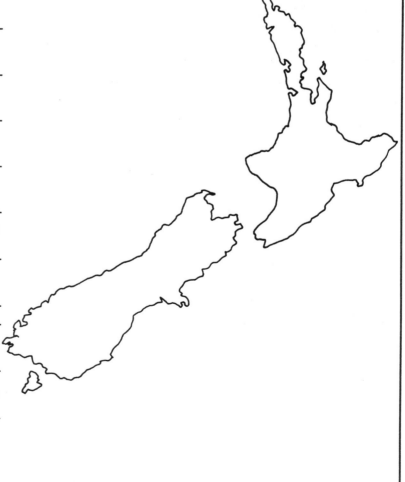

The Middle East:
An Overview for the Teacher

The Middle East has often been called the cradle of civilization and the crossroads for the world's ancient cultures. The Fertile Crescent of Mesopotamia in the Middle East is the place where small hunter-gatherer societies evolved into large, complex, agriculturally-based societies. The list of culture-transforming inventions and innovations that probably arose in the Middle East includes writing, the four-wheeled vehicle, the sailing boat, metallurgy, and a legal system, as well as advances in such intellectual fields as pure and applied science, mathematics, medicine, astronomy, geography, and languages. To heighten student interest in these early civilizations and their accomplishments, let students examine pictures which you have collected of ancient Mesopotamian tools and artifacts. Encourage students to offer tentative interpretations and hypotheses about the early societies based upon their analyses of the pictures.

Identify the Middle East on the globe and have students note its location relative to other regions of the world. Point out to students that the Middle East is where the continents of Africa, Asia, and Europe meet. Throughout history, conquering armies, opportunistic traders, curious scholars, and a multitude of other travelers have crossed the sea and land routes of the Middle East. Because of its unique location, the Middle East played a significant role in the spread and diffusion of ideas across cultures in the ancient world. The Middle East is the birthplace of three major religions—Judaism, Christianity, and Islam—that over time spread throughout the world. Using the political outline map on the following page, make a transparency map of the Middle East. Ask students to identify various countries and other geographic features on the transparency. Label on the map the following countries of the Middle East: Turkey, Cyprus, Israel, Syria, Lebanon, Jordan, Iraq, Iran, Saudi Arabia, Kuwait, Oman, Yemen, the United Arab Emirates, Bahrain, and Qatar. Encourage students to share any information they have about the Middle East.

Today, the Middle East is a land in political and social turmoil. The discovery of vast oil reserves in the region has created economic "haves" and "have nots." Some oil-rich countries like Saudi Arabia, Kuwait, and the United Arab Emirates can afford expensive social programs. Other countries, like Jordan and Yemen, that lack an abundance of mineral resources, are poor. Religious and ethnic conflicts plague the region. Civil war in Lebanon has left that country in ruin. The Arab's opposition to Jewish immigration and aggression against Israel and Israel's displacement of Palestinians and occupation of Arab territory continue to be a major problem in the Middle East. In addition to the Arab-Israeli conflict, Moslem nations in the region have engaged in frequent warfare among themselves. The Iran-Iraq War dragged on for eight bloody years before it ended in a stalemate in 1988. A more recent example is Iraq's attack of Kuwait in 1990 to start the Gulf War, an invasion which was eventually repulsed by the United Nations and the United States.

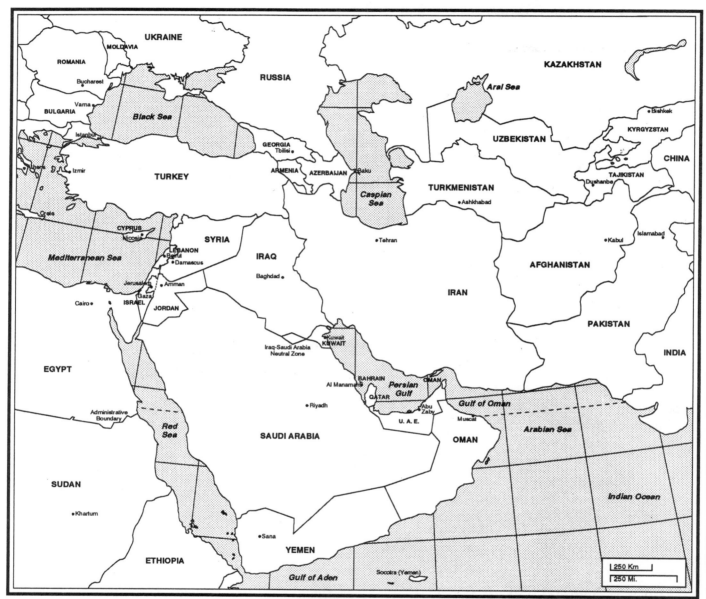

The
Middle East

Kuwait

In the seventeenth century present-day Kuwait was used as a base by Bedouin hunters. The Al-Sabah family has ruled Kuwait since the eighteenth century. It became an independent country in 1961. Today, because of the discovery of huge oil reserves, tiny Kuwait is one of the world's richest countries. Most of Kuwait's oil exports travel by tankers through the Persian Gulf to Japan, Europe, and the United States. Kuwait uses money earned from the sale of oil to fund social programs for its people. The government is attempting to provide a free home for every Kuwaiti family, health care and education for the entire population, and a guaranteed pension for every worker. Unlike American workers, Kuwaitis do not pay an income tax. Kuwait's economic development was halted in 1990 when the country was overrun by Iraqi forces. When the Gulf War ended in 1991, Kuwaitis found to their dismay that the retreating Iraqis had set fire to hundreds of Kuwaiti oil wells. The great waves of black smoke swirling from the fires made midday seem like a moonless night. Today, the oil well fires have long since been extinguished, and Kuwait is rapidly rebuilding its country.

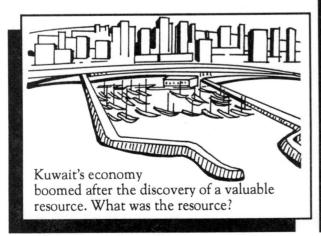

What large body of water borders Kuwait?

INVESTIGATIONS

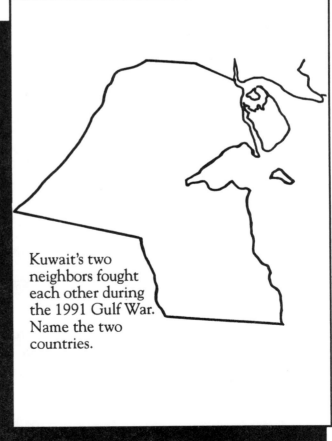

Kuwait's two neighbors fought each other during the 1991 Gulf War. Name the two countries.

Kuwait's economy boomed after the discovery of a valuable resource. What was the resource?

**Curriculum
Connections**

Mathematics: Put the table of Kuwait population on the chalkboard. Ask students to compute the percent of Kuwaitis and non-Kuwaitis in the population in 1961 and 1985. (For your information, the percentages are in parenthesis.) They can make pie graphs showing the percentages for 1961 and 1985. Have students answer the following questions about the population data: Did Kuwait's population increase or decrease between 1961 and 1985? (increase); What was the composition of the population in 1961? (The number of non-Kuwaitis was about equal to that of Kuwaitis by 49.7% to 50.3%.); What was the composition of the population in 1985? (The number of non-Kuwaitis exceeded that of Kuwaitis by 59.9% to 40.1%.); and which group, the non-Kuwaitis or the Kuwaitis, increased at a more rapid rate between 1961 and 1985? (non-Kuwaitis). After students study about oil-rich Kuwait, they should be able to answer this question: Why did the non-Kuwaiti population grow so rapidly? (The rapid rate of economic expansion created by income from Kuwaiti oil provided ample job opportunities and made it necessary to recruit great numbers of foreign workers.)

Nationality	1961 Number	%	1985 Number	%
Kuwaiti	161,909	(50.3)	681,288	(40.1)
Non-Kuwaiti	159,712	(49.7)	1,016,013	(59.9)
Total	321,621	(100)	1,697,301	(100)

Source: Kuwaiti Government

Career Education: The Gulf War focused the attention of the world on Kuwait and the Middle East. Have interested students play the role of a television correspondent covering the war. Their job is to use library resources to describe the events that occurred during the Gulf War between August, 1990, when Iraq invaded Kuwait, and February, 1991, when the Iraqi forces were defeated. The students' brief oral reports should be videotaped if possible for playback to the class. Make certain students are accurate in their reporting, but also encourage them to make the reports as dramatic as possible. Some students might like to accompany their oral reports with drawings they have made of "war scenes" from the front lines.

Art: Write the proverb, "One picture is worth a thousand words," on the chalkboard. Challenge students to draw pictures that "tell" a story about Kuwait.

Economics: The economics of oil can provide students with many concrete examples of such concepts as *scarcity* and *supply* and *demand*. Have students research the leading oil exporting and oil importing nations. Where is much of the world's oil located? Where is much of the world's oil used? After students have gathered a list of oil importers and exporters, ask them to compare and contrast the two groups of nations. How are they alike, and how are they different?

Kuwait Scramble

Unscramble these letters to form answers to the questions below about Kuwait. Put one letter on each line. Put the answers on the blank spaces provided.

A N R D S I

— — — — — —

Y R S E W N E J E

— — — — — — — —

T K I W U A T Y C I

— — — — — — — — —

L T N S N P I I A E A

— — — — — — — — — — —

S M I L A

— — — — —

R R B A N E

— — — — — —

Q R A I

— — — —

1. What is the capital of Kuwait? _____

2. How could you describe most of Kuwait's land? _____

3. What is the nationality of most of Kuwait's oil field workers? _____

4. Which U.S. state is slightly larger than Kuwait? _____

5. Which country does Kuwait face on the north? _____

6. What is the name for Kuwait's money? _____

7. What is the official religion of Kuwait? _____

An Arab Family in Kuwait

There are about 185 million Arabs that live in 18 countries of the Middle East and northern Africa. Use library resources to study the characteristics of an Arab family listed on the chart below. After you have filled in the Arab family section of the chart, fill in the American family section, drawing on information from your own experience.

	Arab Family	American Family
1. Role of men and women in family		
2. Religion		
3. Education		
4. Food		
5. Clothing		
6. Shelter		
7. Transportation		

Iran

In ancient times Iran was known as Persia. With an empire that stretched from Egypt to India, Persia was once the most powerful country in the world. The Islamic religion was brought to Persia by the Arabs, who conquered the region in A.D. 651. In 1935 the Shah, or leader, of Persia renamed the country Iran. The Shah wanted to modernize the country. He introduced Western ideas and used Iran's large oil reserves to stimulate economic growth. But only a few Iranians benefited from the Shah's reforms. Most of the Iranian people remained poor. Many Iranians also did not want to change their traditional ways of life. By the late 1970s, resentment to the Shah's policies became so strong that the people revolted. After the Shah was overthrown, a new government was formed, which was based upon strict Moslem religious law. Today, Iran's future is clouded. A rapidly increasing population and costly war with Iraq have severely strained the nation's resources. Although Iran is an Islamic country, most of the people are not Arabs but descendants of the ancient Persians. They speak a language called *Farsi*.

In 1979 an exiled Islamic leader took over the government of Iran. What was the leader's name?

INVESTIGATIONS

This modern structure is in Iran's capital city. What is the name of the capital?

Carvings of ancient nobles adorn the ruins of Persepolis, which became the capital of the Persian Empire in the sixth century B.C. What famous Persian king built the city?

Current Events: Iran's political policies and actions are frequently in the news. Have students gather newspaper and magazine articles about Iran and then report on their findings. (You can also collect and read articles on Iran to your students.) In their analyses of the news reports, have them consider the following questions: How important is the topic or issue? Are the articles fact- or opinion-oriented? and What themes or topics related to Iran appear most frequently in the news? Also, for each news article, students should try to answer these five questions: who? what? when? where? and why?

Art: Handwoven Persian rugs are world-famous for their quality and beauty. Have students use art books or encyclopedias to research various designs for Persian rugs. Perhaps a local person who is knowledgeable about Persian rugs, like a Persian rug collector or salesperson, could speak to the class on the topic and show students some examples of the smaller rugs. Interested students can use colored markers to copy rug designs on sheets of paper, which can then be displayed on the wall.

Geography: Have students find maps of Iran in an atlas or encyclopedia and draw their own maps of the country on a sheet of poster paper. Their maps should include a legend with symbols representing Iran's capital, Teheran, as well as the following important cities: Qom, Isfahan, Tabriz, Ahvaz, Meshed, and Abadan. Also have them include symbols locating Iran's farming area, industry, livestock, fishing, minerals, and oil. Finally, the following major mountains and bodies of water should be labeled on the map: Zagros Mountains, Elburz Mountains, Kopet-Dag Mountains, Persian Gulf, Strait of Hormuz, Gulf of Oman, Caspian Sea, Lake Urmia, and Karun River.

History: The history of ancient Persia is filled with stories about colorful rulers and exciting military battles. One ruler, Darius the Great, built ancient Persia's most majestic city, Persepolis, the ruins of which stand as a monument to bygone days of power and glory. The Persian Empire once covered an area the size of the United States and reached as far west as present-day Turkey. In the fifth century B.C., only the Greeks stood in the way of Persia's total domination of the region. The Greeks were able to stop the advance of the Persian Army in 490 B.C. at the famous battle of Marathon. Let students create a skit about the battle of Marathon. Students can research the battle and gather information about the military costumes, weapons, and equipment of the ancient Greek and Persian armies. Then they can use large sheets of heavy posterboard and construction paper to make helmets, shields, and weapons to wear in the skit.

Name _____

Iranian Historical Happenings

Important events in Iran's history are described in the left-hand column. The dates of the events are listed in the right-hand column. Use your research skills to match the pairs correctly. Place the correct date on the blank in front of each description.

		Event	Date
_____	1.	Reza Khan became shah (ruler)	1925
_____	2.	The Iran-Iraq War was fought	1500s B.C.
_____	3.	Cyrus the Great founded the Persian Empire	1941
_____	4.	Mongols invaded Iran	1794
_____	5.	The Shah was overthrown and Iran became an Islamic Republic	331 B.C.
_____	6.	Safavid dynasty began	1980-88
_____	7.	Alexander the Great conquered the Persians	1501
_____	8.	Aryans began their migration to Iran	550 B.C.
_____	9.	Sassanid dynasty began	1220
_____	10.	Mohammed Reza Pahlavi became shah	224
_____	11.	Arabs conquered Iran	1989
_____	12.	Iran's first constitution was signed	1906
_____	13.	Qajars dynasty began	1979
_____	14.	Ayatollah Khomeini died	Mid-600s

Iran Crossword

Use your research skills to find the answers to this crossword puzzle about Iran.

Across
1. The chief product of Iran's fishing industry
3. Iran is slightly larger than this American state
4. Iranian rulers were once called by this name
5. U.S. president who dealt with the Iranian hostage crisis
8. Iran's first leader after 1979 revolution
9. This group conquered Iran in the seventh century A.D.
11. This word is enscribed on Iran's flag.
14. This is what Iranian houses of worship are called.
17. Most of Iran consists of mountains and _____.
18. In the 1980's Iran fought this country

Down
1. Most of Iran's population lives near this sea
2. This is a popular Iranian food.
6. This is the capital of Iran.
7. The name of an ancient ruins
9. "Iran" means "land of the _ _ _ _ _ _ _."
10. Iran's most important mineral
12. Iran faces this country on the northwest.
13. A traditional garment worn by Iranian women.
15. Most Iranians are members of this religion.
16. This is the official language of Iran.

Iraq

Iraq is a country with a glorious past. Present-day Iraq was once known as Mesopotamia, which means the land between the two rivers in Greek. Around 3500 B.C. the world's earliest civilization, founded by the Sumerians, arose along the shores of two rivers, the Tigris and the Euphrates. The two rivers never ran dry, and their flooding made the soils fertile. The Sumerians were probably the first people in the world to develop systems of agriculture, writing, and government. For these reasons, Mesopotamia is often called the "cradle of civilization." The Babylonians ruled most of Meso-potamia by 1700 B.C. The most important Babylonian ruler was Hammurabi—The Law Giver. He was the first person to organize a system of laws and penalties to govern society. These laws, which were engraved on clay tablets, have come to be known as the *Code of Hammurabi*. Today, about a quarter of the Iraqi people are farmers or herders. The rest are involved in such areas as industry, mining, fishing, manufacturing, trade, and the military. Iraq is considered to have one of the richest oil fields in the world. But much of Iraq's oil resources have been used recently to pay for bloody wars with Iran and Kuwait.

Zawra Tower is located in Iraq's capital and largest city. What is the city's name?

INVESTIGATIONS

Most of Iraq's people live along the country's two major rivers. What are names of the two rivers?

Copper trays and pitchers along with a vast variety of Oriental items are found in Iraq's markets. By what name are these rows of shops called?

Curriculum Connections

Geography: Students can use encyclopedias, atlases, and other reference sources to locate information about the major geographic features of Iraq. Have students identify major mountains, rivers, roads, railways, cities, crops (including fruit, grain, rice, and cotton), and oil fields. Students can trace a map of Iraq on sheets of posterboard and draw symbols on the map to represent the geographic features. Encourage students to illustrate their maps with pictures of the Iraqi flag or coat of arms.

Diet and Health: Meat, vegetables, rice, wheat, and fruit are each a basic part of the Iraqi diet. Popular Iraqi dishes include the following: *kubba*, a wheat-minced mixture which is stuffed with meat and filled with nuts, spices, parsley, and onion that are then formed into balls and boiled; *dolma*, made from vine leaves, cabbage, lettuce, onions, eggplants, cucumbers, rice, and minced meat; and *kebab*, consisting of minced meat on skewers grilled on a charcoal fire, which is usually served with salad and an Iraqi flat bread. Consult a cook book for Iraqi and Middle Eastern recipes to share with the class.

Technology: Many Iraqi farmers still use the same tools and practices that were used in ancient times. Have students research ancient Middle Eastern agricultural methods and compare them with modern approaches. They can make charts, entitled "Ancient" and "Modern," to display the gathered information.

International Affairs: Iraq attacked Kuwait in August, 1990. The Iraqi leader, Saddam Hussein, claiming Kuwait was legally a part of Iraq, declared that he had annexed it. Have interested students investigate Iraqi and Kuwaiti history to determine if there were any basis for this claim. Students can also trace the diplomatic and military actions taken by the United Nations and the United States in response to Iraqi aggression.

Archeology: The ancient ruins of Mesopotamia attest to the grandeur of the early cities' art and architecture. Have students research the various early civilizations, including the Sumerians, Akkadians, Assyrians, Chaldeans, Arabs, and Abbassids. Make certain students note the skillful way early towns were laid out. Most were surrounded by strong ramparts and contained within them towers and temples decorated with paintings, mosaics, and sculpture. Each city had its own *ziggurats*, or raised platforms upon which temples were built. As successive levels were added, these ziggurats took the form of gigantic spiral towers.

Literature: The famous *Arabian Nights* or *The Thousand and One Nights* introduced the world to such renowned characters as Aladdin, Ali Baba, and Sinbad. Read one of the stories to the class and have students discuss the virtues and faults of the various characters. Does the story give them any insights about personal qualities the early Arabian people might have admired or detested?

Facts and Figures About Iraq

Name _____

Use the pool of words at the bottom of the page and library resources to find the facts and figures about Iraq that are missing from the passage below. Fill in the blank spaces with the correct answers. (Please note that there are more words in the pool than blank spaces in the passage.)

Iraq is located in the northeastern part of the _____ (1) Peninsula. The southwestern part of the country is mainly _____ (2). In contrast, southeastern Iraq consists of a _____ (3) plain. At the center, the terrain changes to _____ (4) grasslands. The northeastern part of the nation is _____ (5). Iraq's two great rivers, the _____ (6) and the _____ (7), originate in this region. In southern Iraq, these two rivers unite to form the mighty _____ (8) River. The country has an area of _____ (9) square miles. Iraq's population is about _____ (10) million. The capital of Iraq is _____ (11). Most of the Iraqi people are _____ (12), although a sizable minority, called the _____ (13), live in the northern part of the country. Iraq's number one natural resource is _____ (14). Among the country's chief agricultural products are _____ (15) and _____ (16).

Kurds	fertile	Arabs	corn
Baghdad	Shatt-al-Arab	Tigris	cotton
20	50	169,235	98,432
dates	oil	wool	gold
mountainous	rolling	Arabian	Iberian
swampy	Euphrates	Nile	desert

Cradle of Civilization

It is hard to imagine life without the inventions and innovations developed by the early civilizations that arose in present-day Iraq. In the space provided on the right, list contemporary examples of tools and activities which are related to the past achievements listed on the left below. For example, the past achievement of the invention of writing is related to the modern-day "pencil," which is a tool, as well as to the contemporary activity of "writing poetry."

Past Achievements

Modern-day Examples of Relationships

1. Writing is invented.

2. Potters wheel is invented.

3. Techniques of metal smelting, glazing, and welding are discovered.

Saudi Arabia

The Kingdom of Saudi Arabia was established in 1932. Since then, the nation has witnessed dramatic economic development thanks to the discovery beneath the desert sand of the world's richest oil reserve. Today, Saudi Arabia is the world's largest exporter of oil and natural gas. The kingdom is ruled by the Saud family, which believes it has a "legacy as guardian of a nation deeply rooted in Islam." There is no constitution or legislature. Saudi Arabia's legal system is based upon the teachings of Islam. Saudi Arabia is very important in the Muslim world because it is the birthplace of Islam. Each year, millions of pilgrims come to Saudi Arabia to worship at the holy city of Mecca. According to Islam, all Muslims—and there are about a billion around the world—must make this visit at least once. Because of Saudi Arabia's wealth from oil, the nation has been able to engage in expensive development programs, such as the construction of desalination plants to convert seawater for drinking and industrial uses. Irrigation and other farming technologies are making Saudi Arabia a substantial producer of wheat, corn, barley, livestock, and poultry. The nation also provides its citizens with high-quality medical care, social services, and educational facilities.

Camel racing is a traditional sport of a group of migrating herders who live in Saudi Arabia. What are these nomads called?

INVESTIGATIONS

Most Saudi Arabian people are Muslims, which means they practice Islam, a major religion of the Middle East. Where do Muslims go to worship?

The Moslem creed is inscribed in Arabic on Saudi Arabia's flag. What does the creed say?

Sports: Have students compare the traditional and modern sports of Saudi Arabia with the United States'. The swift saluki hound, named for an ancient city in southern Arabia, was once used to hunt Arabian ibex, gazelle, rabbit, and lynx. Falconry is a traditional sport that is still practiced. Horse and camel racing are other traditional sports still popular today. Popular modern sports in Saudi Arabia include track, soccer, and swimming. Some of the world's most beautiful coral reefs for skin divers and snorkelers are located beneath the Red Sea and the Persian Gulf.

Science: Have interested students research the famous Arabian horse and find out why it is one of the world's most sought-after breeds. They can locate information on the following topics: the history of the horses, why the horses are famous, what the horses eat, how to care for the horses, how the Arabian breed is different from other breeds, and how the horses are trained.

Mathematics: Arab traders spread the Arabic numeral system across the Mediterranean region. This system, which is based on 10 numerals, is used today throughout the world. Students can practice writing the Arabic system in the Arabic language by copying the numerals below.

٩	٨	٧	٦	٥	٤	٣	٢	١	٠
9	8	7	6	5	4	3	2	1	0

Religion: Have interested students study about the life of Muhammad, the founder of Islam. They can write short biographies of Muhammad that include information about his birth around the year A.D. 570 in Mecca, Allah's messages to him, his emigration to Madinah, and his destruction of the idols in the *Ka'abah*. Information about the *Koran*, the holy book of Islam, should also be included in their biographies.

Language Arts: The Arabic language is the official language of many countries in the Middle East, including Iraq, Kuwait, and Saudi Arabia. Arabic is written from left to right or from the top of the page to the bottom. Some English words like *algebra* and *magazine* come from Arabic. Have students use dictionaries to identify other English words that come from Arabic. Let students practice writing the Arabic alphabet presented here.

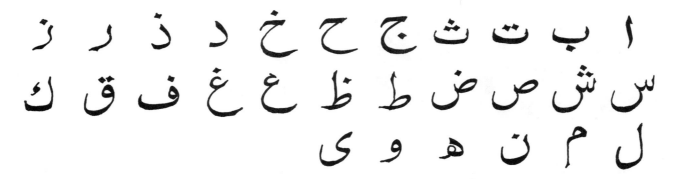

The Arabian Peninsula

Of the six countries that lie on the Arabian Peninsula, Saudi Arabia is by far the largest. Use a map of the Arabian Peninsula in an encyclopedia or atlas to find the locations of the places described by the clues below. Write the names of the places on the blank spaces beneath each clue. Then plot and label the places on the outline map below.

1. This tiny country is off the coast.

   _____

2. This is the largest country.

   _____

3. This country occupies the southernmost part of the peninsula.

   _____

4. This country is between Iraq and Saudi Arabia.

   _____

5. The capital of Saudi Arabia is located here.

   _____

6. Abu Dhabi is the capital of this country.

   _____

7. This country is on the Arabian Peninsula's southeastern corner.

   _____

8. This country is on a peninsula in the Persian Gulf.

   _____

9. Muslim pilgrims visit this holy city.

   _____

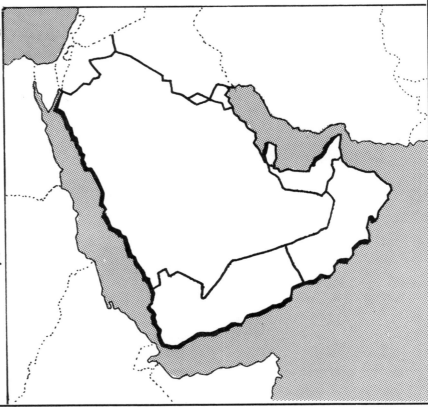

Name _____

The Five Pillars of Islam

Historically, Saudi Arabia has occupied a special place in the Islamic world. Five times a day millions of Moslems everywhere turn to Mecca, the birthplace of Islam and the Prophet Muhammad, to pray. Another Islamic holy city in Saudi Arabia is Madinah, Muhammad's burial place. Islam has five basic obligations, or "Pillars of Faith," which are listed below in Arabic and English, that each Moslem must fulfill in his or her lifetime. Use library resources to reseach the five pillars of Islam. Then use the space provided below to write a paragraph about each one.

1. *Shahadah* (profession of faith)

2. *Salat* (ritual prayer)

3. *Zakat* (almsgiving)

4. *Sawn* (fasting)

5. *Hajj* (visit to the revered place)

Israel

Israel was created in 1948 as the homeland for the Jewish people. Since then, Jewish immigrants from throughout the world have settled in this small, triangular-shaped country. Located along the eastern shore of the Mediterranean Sea, present-day Israel has a long and troubled history. Called Palestine in ancient times, the land has been conquered by Hebrews, Babylonians, Persians, Greeks, Romans, Arabs, Crusaders, Ottomans, and the British. After Israel was established, the Arab majority who then lived there, called Palestinians, violently opposed the Jewish immigration. Many Palestinians fled to neighboring Arab countries. Over the years, Israel has fought a series of wars with the Palestinians and their Arab allies. Today, 83 percent of Israel's population is Jewish, and the displacement of Palestinians continues to be a major problem in the Middle East. In 1993 Israel signed a peace agreement with the Palestinians that granted Palestinian self-rule in some of the lands occupied by Israel. Israel's highly educated population has used modern technology to turn the country's arid inland area into a productive agricultural region. The chief crops are citrus fruit and vegetables. Included among Israel's most important industries are diamond cutting, textiles, electronics, and food processing.

What is the symbol on the flag of Israel called?

INVESTIGATIONS

In 1979 Egypt and Israel made peace after discussions in the United States with this U.S. President. What was his name?

The official emblem of Israel displays the ancient symbol of the Jewish people. What is the symbol called? The symbol is linked at the bottom by the word *Israel*, which is inscribed in the official language. What is the official language of Israel?

History: Conflict between Arabs and Jews is one of the main reasons why the Middle East continues to be one of the world's most volatile regions. After you have provided students with the brief historical overview presented here, have them investigate specific aspects of Israel's past in more detail. In the late 1800s, after centuries of persecution in Europe, a movement known as *Zionism* called for the establishment of a Jewish homeland in Palestine. Jewish immigration to Palestine increased after World War I, when Britain, which supported the Zionist movement, gained control of the region. In the 1930s great numbers of Jews fled Europe to escape Nazi persecution in Germany. The Nazis, in what was to become known as the *Holocaust*, killed over 6 million Jews during World War II. After World War II, the United Nations proposed that Palestine be divided into an Arab state and a Jewish state. Although Palestinian Arabs rejected the United Nations plan, Israel was established in 1948. Immediately thereafter, fighting between Arab and Jewish sides erupted. Neighboring Arab nations attacked Israel with the intention of destroying it, but they were defeated instead. Despite a series of wars with its Arab neighbors, Israel has managed not only to survive, but to gain control of Arab land, including the Golan Heights, and the West Bank. Israel's unwillingness to give up all of its Arab territories is a major source of contention between the two sides today. An important step toward peace was taken in 1993 when Israel agreed to give Palestinians self-rule in the Gaza strip and Jericho.

Ecology: Israel has received high marks for its commitment to environmental protection. With few natural resources on which to draw, Israel has developed environment-friendly technologies to increase food and energy production. An innovative drip irrigation system conserves water and produces high crop yields. Israel is the world's largest consumer of solar energy relative to total energy consumption. Israel has even come up with an oil-eating bacteria for oil spills. After students research some of the many Israeli ecological accomplishments, they can write paragraphs about whether or not they believe Israel's innovations can be used as a model for other countries.

Religion: The city of Jerusalem is a holy place to three major world religions: Judaism, Christianity, and Islam. The Wailing Wall, which is the last remnant of a holy temple from Biblical times, is sacred to the Jews. The Al-Aqsa mosque, which is the traditional site of the Prophet Muhammad's ascent to heaven, is considered to be one of Islam's three most holy places. Jerusalem is also the site of a number of places associated with the life of Jesus, including the Garden of Gethsemane and the Church of the Holy Sepulchre. Have students compare and contrast these three religions. They can report their findings to the class.

Social Organization: Israel's 270 rural communal societies, called *kibbutzim*, are scattered throughout Israel. Each kibbutz has a population of around 500–600. Have students research these unique communities which exemplify both democracy and socialism in action.

Israel Word Puzzle

Fill in the answers to the clues listed on the left by placing one letter on each line on the right.

1. Israel's type of government.   _ _ _ _ _ _ _ ☐

2. This is the name of foods prepared according to Jewish dietary law.   _ ☐ _ _ _ _

3. Israel's capital   _ _ _ _ _ _ _ ☐

4. This is the name of Israel's parliament.   ☐ _ _ _ _ _

5. This is Israel's major industrial center. (two words)   _ _ _ _ _ ☐ _

6. This is the region where most of the people live. (two words)   _ _ _ _ _ _ ☐ _ _ _ _

7. This is Israel's most important mineral resource.   ☐ _ _ _ _

8. Many Israelis live in these cooperative communities.   _ _ _ _ ☐ _ _ _ _

9. This is Israel's longest river.   _ _ ☐ _ _ _

10. What is Israel's most sacred holy day? If your answers above are correct, the letters inside the boxes above will provide you with the two-word answer to this question. Put your answer on the lines below.

___ ___ ___ ___   ___ ___ ___ ___ ___ ___

Name _____

In and Around Israel

Read the clues below about places in and around Israel. You can use a map of Israel in an encyclopedia or atlas to locate the places. Then write the names of the places on the blank spaces provided, and label them on the map below.

1. This country is southwest of Israel.

   _____

2. This place is the lowest spot on earth.

   _____

3. Three major religions consider this city a holy place.

   _____

4. A peace agreement in 1993 placed this narrow strip of land under Palestinian self-rule.

   _____

5. This country is directly north of Israel.

   _____

6. Syria wants this place, taken by Israel in 1967, back.

   _____

7. Israel's major seaport is located here.

   _____

8. This country is directly east of Israel.

   _____

9. This body of water provides Israel with its only access to the Red Sea.

   _____

10. This place, seized from Jordan, has been occupied by Israel since 1967.

    _____

Africa:

An Overview for the Teacher

Africa is a tremendously diverse region. It is the home of over 800 different ethnic groups, each with its own language and cultural traditions, scattered across an ever-changing landscape of deserts, mountains, plains, coasts, and rain forests, each with its distinct plant and animal life.

Identify Africa on a globe and have students note its location and size relative to other regions of the world. Africa is huge. The second largest continent, it covers almost 21 percent of the world's total surface area. The Sahara Desert alone is larger than the continental United States. On a map of Africa (you can make a transparency from the political map of Africa on the next page), trace Africa's relatively smooth coastline. Point out to the students that even though Africa is almost three times larger than Europe, Europe's irregular coastline is more than twice as long as Africa's, which has few bays or peninsulas. Tell students that Africa is an immense plateau. In fact, a cross-section of Africa's landscape from coast to coast would look much like an inverted saucer. Next, let students find the following major rivers of Africa: Nile (which is the world's longest at 4,145 miles), Congo (or Zaire, 2,716 miles), Niger (2,600 miles), and Zambezi (1,700 miles). Point out to students that only parts of Africa's rivers are navigable to large boats.

Much of Africa's history is about European domination and exploitation. The Portuguese came first in the late 1400s and found a rich "land of gold." Other European nations arrived shortly thereafter, and soon there were gold and slave trading posts established along the coast of West Africa. By the early 1500s the Portuguese had a foothold in East Africa, where they vied with the Arabs over control of the coastal area. Over the next few hundred years an estimated 10 million Africans were forced into bondage. In the nineteenth century Europeans began to explore the vast interior of Africa. The grab for Africa intensified in the late 1800s, and by 1914 almost all of Africa was under European colonial rule. European control of Africa started to unravel in 1957 when Britain was forced to turn the Suez Canal over to Egypt. By the end of the 1960s, most African colonies had gained their independence.

Today, Africa faces many problems. Among the most serious are conflicts over political boundaries, ethnic conflicts, inequality, corrupt and undemocratic governments, dependence on one or two export products, unemployment, foreign debt, overpopulation in some areas, poverty, famine, disease, low productivity, inadequate infrastructure, and lack of entrepreneurial and technical skills.

There is hope for the future. With an abundance of rich mineral resources and a high potential for hydroelectric power, it is possible for Africa to move forward. Many countries are currently making economic and political reforms which, hopefully, will eventually bring prosperity and freedom to their people.

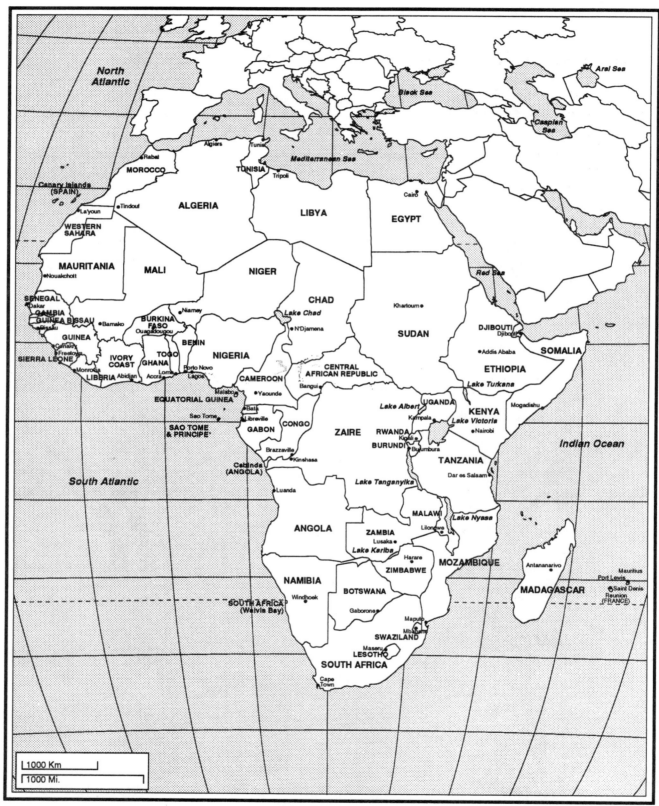

Africa

94

Egypt

When you think about Egypt, things like the Great Pyramid at Giza, the largest human-made structure ever built, or King Tut's tomb, filled with priceless treasures of gold and jewels, probably come to mind. For thousands of years, Egypt was one of the most powerful and advanced civilizations in the ancient world. Many of the monuments that the Egyptian pharaohs (or rulers) built to glorify themselves and their gods still stand majestically in the desert. Today, millions of tourists come to marvel at these wonders of the world. Some also take a ride on a camel. These "ships of the desert" have carried people and goods across the sands of the Sahara for centuries. The Nile River made the ancient Egyptian civilization possible. Besides bringing lifegiving water, the river's annual floods created the fertile land along its banks. The Nile region is now one of the most densely populated places in the world. Egypt's rapidly increasing population is one of the nation's biggest problems. Egypt is a major producer of cotton and textiles. Other important industries include petrochemicals, cement, mining, and manufacturing.

INVESTIGATIONS

What is the name of this giant statue built 4,500 years ago that has the body of a lion and a human head?

The longest river in the world cuts through Egypt. What is the river's name and how long is it?

Thousands of years ago, gold masks were used to cover the heads of dead Egytian rulers. What were these rulers called?

Curriculum Connections

Careers: After studying about pyramids, tombs, and treasures, some students may be interested in learning more about the career choice of people who investigate ancient cultures for a living. Archeology is a branch of anthropology that attempts to reconstruct history from the remains of ancient human cultures, especially those cultures lacking a written record. Archeologists make inferences about ancient people by studying the cultural materials they left behind, such as tools, pieces of pottery, or even garbage. They try to answer questions like the following: What were the daily life and customs of the people like? or Why does a culture change over time? Archeologists do not mind getting their hands dirty. They spend considerable time at excavation sites all over the world digging for evidence, making precise measurements, and taking careful field notes. Archeologists who specialize in the study of ancient Egypt are often called Egyptologists. Encourage interested students to investigate the profession of archeology and report their findings to the class.

Geography: After students have made their models of pyramids (see "Building a Pyramid" student activity), small groups of four or five students can incorporate the models into a scenic representation, or diorama, of ancient Egypt. The students can construct other miniatures for their diorama. Let students consult books with illustrations of ancient Egypt for ideas about appropriate figures and objects to include. Each group will need a large box to display the exhibit. Sand can be used to make the landscape as realistic as possible. Encourage students to create a painted background for the diorama that blends in with the scenic representations in the foreground.

Religion: At the core of Egypt's ancient civilization was religion. The Egyptians believed in many gods. Among the most important were: Re or Amon-re, the sun god and chief deity; Osiris, god of vegetation and the dead; Isis, goddess of the devoted mother and wife; Horus, god of the sky; and Ptah, the creator god of Memphis, the capital of ancient Egypt. The Egyptians believed that just about everything that happened to them was caused by the gods. The Egyptians also believed in life after death. In preparation for the afterlife, Egyptians would mummify, or embalm, the body and place it in a tomb, which was filled with many of the dead person's most important material possessions and necessities, such as jewels, clothing, food, utensils, and even toys. Assign small groups of four or five students the task of researching one of the Egyptian gods. The groups can illustrate their reports with pictures of the gods, as well as with drawings of items found in the tombs. When the groups give their reports, have students speculate about why certain items were included in the tombs.

Language Arts: Students can use encyclopedias and other library resources to research the Egyptian system of writing called *hieroglyphics*.

Egypt's Three Kingdoms

The history of ancient Egypt is divided into three periods: the Old Kingdom (2700 B.C. to 2200 B.C.), the Middle Kingdom (2000 B.C. to 1800 B.C.), and the New Kingdom (1550 B.C. to 331 B.C.). Below are listed some statements. Each of the statements is true about one of the three ancient Egyptian kingdoms. Use library resources to correctly match the statement with the kingdom. Write the statement inside the box under the appropriate kingdom.

Old Kingdom:	Middle Kingdom:	New Kingdom:

Statements:

1. The peak of Egypt's power

2. Queen Hatshepsut ruled.

3. Alexander the Great conquered Egypt.

4. The largest pyramids were built.

5. King Tutankhamen (Tut) was pharaoh.

6. The Egyptians learned to build ocean-going ships made of cedar.

7. Egypt was controlled for a time by the Hyksos.

8. Memphis was the first capital of this kingdom.

9. Amenemhet ruled.

10. Ramses II ruled.

11. Trade between Egypt and Palestine started.

12. The first pyramid was built.

Building a Pyramid

"Huge" cannot begin to describe the giant pyramids the Egyptians built along the Nile. The largest was the Great Pyramid at Giza, which took 100,000 workers about 20 years to build. With the following clues, make some monumental mathematical calculations about this awesome structure in the space provided below. Then follow the directions below to build it.

_____1. The pyramid covers as much land as 12 football fields. Approximately how many acres does it cover?

_____2. About 2.3 million blocks of limestone were used to build the pyramid. Each block weighed about 2.5 tons. What was the pyramid's approximate total weight?

_____3. The pyramid has a square ground plan. Each side of the square is about 750 feet long. The outside walls of the pyramid form four triangles that meet at a point that is about 500 feet high. Use pieces of cardboard to construct a model of the pyramid based on the following scale: 1 inch equals 100 feet.

_____4. Before you construct your pyramid, make a scale drawing of one side of the pyramid on a separate piece of paper.

Calculations:

Morocco

Situated in northwestern Africa, Morocco lies along the Atlantic and Mediterranean coasts. About the size of California, Morocco is a land of geographic contrasts. The snow-capped Atlas Mountains stretch across much of the country. To the south is the barren Sahara Desert. Scattered here and there are fertile valleys with fields of barley, corn, and wheat, or fig and citrus orchards. Along the Atlantic coast are sandy beaches. Almost all of the Moroccan people are Arabs or Berbers who practice the Islamic religion. Most of the people farm or raise cattle, sheep, or goats. Morocco's largest cities are Rabat (the capital), Casablanca, and Marrakech. In the old sections of Morocco's cities are narrow, winding streets, white-walled houses, and beautiful mosques with towering minarets. On Friday, Islam's holy day, a religious person in the minaret calls the Moroccans to the mosque for prayer. In the marketplaces are many small shops, each one selling a specialty such as fresh fruit and dates, gold and silver jewelry, rugs or, of course, Morocco's world-famous leather goods.

INVESTIGATIONS

This is a busy marketplace in Marrakech where traditional Moroccan crafts are sold. What is Morocco's chief export?

What major North African mountain range looks down on the ancient oasis-cities of Morocco?

These Moroccan musicians are dressed in tradiional garments. What are the original inhabitants of Morocco called?

Curriculum Connections

Cooperative Learning: In this activity, called "Jig-Saw," small cooperative groups of six students will piece together information about the culture of Morocco's Arab and Berber people. Assign each student in a cooperative group one of the following topics on the Arabs and Berbers to research: religion, family life, education, food, work, and clothing/shelter. After all of the students in the groups have done their initial library research on their assigned topics and written the information down on note cards, they are ready to be placed in "expert" groups, which is the first phase of the "Jig-Saw" activity. Each expert group is comprised of students from the cooperative groups who have researched the same topic. For example, the students from the different cooperative groups who researched religion would form one expert group, and the students who researched family life another group, and so on. The purpose of each expert group is to let students who researched the same topic share information and clarify their understanding of the topic. Let students stay in their expert groups until they seem to have a good grasp of the topic. When students have completed their interaction in the expert groups, it is time for the second phase of "Jig-Saw." In this phase of the activity, students return to their cooperative groups to share their areas of expertise with one another. It is each cooperative group member's responsibility to listen carefully and record the basic information presented by the other members of the group so that, upon completion of the six presentations, all of the members of the group have basic information recorded on all six topics about Arab and Berber culture. When the groups have completed the second phase, a spokesperson for each group can share the group's findings with the class.

Geography: Have students plot latitude and longitude coordinates for places in Morocco. Using a globe and string, let them measure the distance between Casablanca and their own community. Ask them to determine the day and time in their own community when it is 1:00 a.m., Saturday, in Morocco.

History: Only eight miles of water separates Morocco, in Africa, from Spain, in Europe. Let interested students investigate the historical connections and contacts between the people of these two great regions of the world.

Science: Phosphate rock is Morocco's biggest export. Challenge students to find out more about this mineral. Ask them to identify the various processed products that can be made from phosphate rock.

International Affairs: At the moment a dispute is raging over the control of Western Sahara, a land to which Morocco has had a long-term claim. Invite interested students to investigate the current status of the dispute and report their findings to the class.

Morocco in a Nutshell

Below is a passage about Morocco, but some key facts have been left out. Your job is to use library resources to track down the missing information. Put the correct facts on the blank spaces.

The population of Morocco is approximately _____ (1) million. About _____ (2) percent of the people live in urban areas. Morocco's type of government is called a _____ (3). The government is headed by a _____ (4). Most of the Moroccans are either Arabs or _____ (5). The official language of the nation is _____(6). In the towns the people congregate at the outdoor market, which is called a _____ (7) in Arabic. At the marketplace they talk and barter for goods. A traditional red, brimless felt cap, called a _____ (8), is worn by many of the men on some formal occasions. Moroccan women who follow _____ (9) tradition wear veils to cover their faces. The national food or dish of Morocco is called _____ (10). It is made of steamed wheat dough which is served with vegetables, meat, or fish in a soupy broth. The main occupation of the people is _____ (11). Most of Morocco's crops are grown in the _____ (12) region. Some chief crops are grain, fruits, and _____(13). Mining is an important part of Morocco's economy. Morocco is the world's biggest exporter of _____ (14). Moroccans are noted for their fine handicraft work. Morocco is especially famous worldwide for the quality of its products made from _____ (15).

Mapping Morocco

A trip around Morocco would take you near snow-capped mountains, through valleys, along the seacoast, and into the barren desert. To use the map below as a guide for such a trip, you will need to fill in a few important geographic details. Use a map of Morocco from an atlas or encyclopedia to locate the geographic features listed below. Then design a legend that includes symbols for the features and draw them on the outline map.

Geographic Features:

Capital city
Casablanca
Rif Mountains
Meknes
Fez

Marrakech
Strait of Gibraltar
Atlas Mountains
Mediterranean Sea
Tangier

Ghana

Ghana, which is located on the west coast of Africa, was called the *Gold Coast* by the early Portuguese who struck gold there in 1471. For hundreds of years Europeans fought over control of Ghana's resources. They built forts and castles along the coast of Ghana to serve as trading posts, and they sent hordes of merchants there for gold and slaves. Today, although Ghana is an independent nation, its economy is very weak. The price of Ghana's biggest export, *cocoa*, which is used to make chocolate, has dropped. Many Ghanaians cannot find work, and some of the well-educated people have left the country. To get the economy moving, the government is encouraging foreign companies to invest in Ghana. The nation has valuable minerals, fish and forest resources, and the potential to develop abundant hydro-electric power. If companies and businesses are started, there will be more jobs for Ghanaians. Ghana also wants more tourists to visit. There are a number of animal reserves spread across the country. Ghana is trying to increase its wildlife population, which was reduced to low levels in the past by hunting.

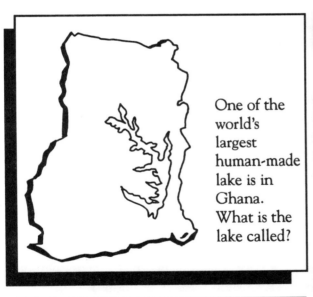

One of the world's largest human-made lake is in Ghana. What is the lake called?

INVESTIGATIONS

Females who belong to Ghana's largest and most powerful ethnic group carry wooden dolls similar to this one. What is the name of the ethnic group?

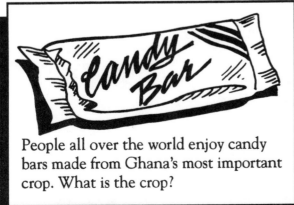

People all over the world enjoy candy bars made from Ghana's most important crop. What is the crop?

Curriculum Connections

Literature and Drama: In Ghana, as in other parts of Africa, the professional storyteller played a very important role in traditional village life. This is because it was the storyteller who imparted the wisdom of the ages from one generation to the next. In Ghana, every village had its own storyteller. In the evening the villagers, especially young people, would gather in a circle around a fire and listen to the storyteller. Among the folk tales the storyteller would recite were the many adventures of Spider—stories about how the Spider got a thin waist, why it lives in ceilings, or how it got a bald head. Ghanaian children love these stories, probably because the clever and mischievous Spider always outwits its bigger and stronger friends. The best storytellers were also great actors. They could imitate the sound of rain or the roar of a leopard. Your students would enjoy listening to some Ghanaian folk tales. Perhaps you have some budding young actors (male or female) in your class who would like to take the part of the storyteller. Most school and community libraries have one or more books on Ghanaian and West African folk tales, such as Joyce C. Arkhurst's *The Adventures of Spider*, published by Little, Brown, and Company.

Science: The most important cash crop of Ghana is cocoa. Although most American students are quite familiar with the chocolate which comes from cocoa, they often know very little about the cocoa plant itself. Ghanaian farmers plant dried cocoa beans just before the start of the rainy season. The cocoa trees must grow five years before they are mature enough to produce bean pods that can be harvested. After the white beans are removed from the ripe pods, they are covered with leaves and left to ferment for about a week. Next the beans, which by now have turned brown, are placed on racks to dry in the sun. The dried beans are then bagged, weighed, and sold to government buyers for export. Much of the cocoa is exported to the chocolate-loving countries of Western Europe and North America, where it is transformed into candy and other food products. Assign students the task of researching this fascinating and tasty plant.

Art: Ghana's largest ethnic group, the Ashanti, are well known for their weaving and wood carving. Ashanti weavers are noted for *kente* cloths. This colorful and intricately designed cloth, made from silk yarn, is the Ghanaian national dress. Some kente cloth owned by Ghanaian chiefs are so valuable they are worn only on special occasions. The Ashanti are also famous for their wooden stools and dolls. The stools, which are made from solid pieces of wood, are carved in different shapes and designs for everyone in Ashanti society. There are special stool designs for chiefs. Like the stools, the dolls are carved from a single piece of wood. The *akuaba* doll, as it is called, was traditionally used both as a toy for girls to play with, and as an object in which resides magical powers for women to carry with them to ensure that they would have children. Show students pictures of these Ashanti artifacts and let them design their own *kente* cloth, stools, and dolls.

Ghana Time Line

An assortment of important events in Ghana's history are listed below. Match the event to the year(s) it happened by putting the letter next to the event inside the box next to the date on the time line along the bottom of the page. Like any good historian, you'll need to consult some library resources before you put the events and dates together.

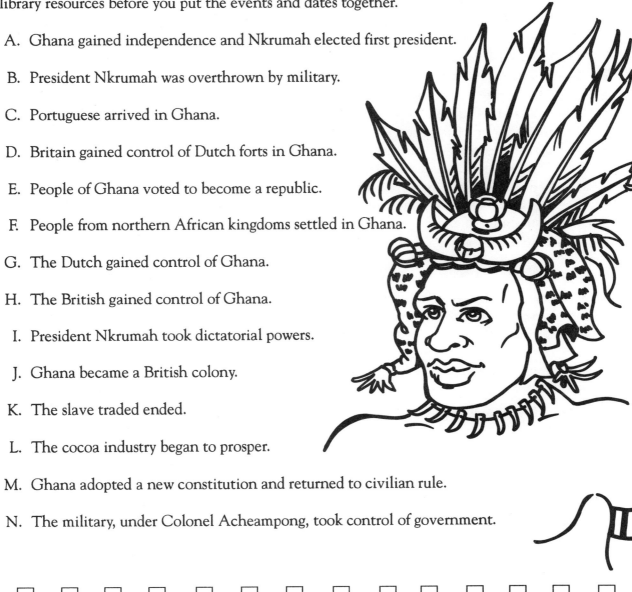

A. Ghana gained independence and Nkrumah elected first president.

B. President Nkrumah was overthrown by military.

C. Portuguese arrived in Ghana.

D. Britain gained control of Dutch forts in Ghana.

E. People of Ghana voted to become a republic.

F. People from northern African kingdoms settled in Ghana.

G. The Dutch gained control of Ghana.

H. The British gained control of Ghana.

I. President Nkrumah took dictatorial powers.

J. Ghana became a British colony.

K. The slave traded ended.

L. The cocoa industry began to prosper.

M. Ghana adopted a new constitution and returned to civilian rule.

N. The military, under Colonel Acheampong, took control of government.

☐ ☐ ☐ ☐ ☐ ☐ ☐ ☐ ☐ ☐ ☐ ☐ ☐ ☐
1200s 1471 1642 1850s 1860s 1872 1886 1900s 1957 1960 1964 1966 1969 1972

Name _____

Investing in Ghana

In this group activity you and the other members of your group are to portray a group of American investors who are meeting to decide on the best possible kind of company to establish in Ghana. After your group reaches a decision, the group can present a report to the class with a rationale which explains the decision. But before your group decides what to do, the following factors should be researched and considered:

1. The geographic location of Ghana.
2. The shipping routes between Ghana and major world markets.
3. Ghana's climate and topography.
4. The availability, education/training, and receptivity of the Ghanaians.
5. The major geographic features of Ghana, including population centers.
6. The kinds of established businesses and industries in Ghana.
7. The opportunities for education in Ghana.
8. The opportunities for recreation in Ghana.
9. The number of employees needed in the new company.
10. The availability of energy sources.
11. The availability of natural resources.

Of all the factors listed above, perhaps the most crucial for a new company is the availability of natural resources. Below is a list of Ghana's major raw materials. To make a wise decision about the kind of company you want, your group will need to make a list of the processed products that can be made from each of the raw materials.

Ghana's Raw Materials

1. Cattle, sheep, goats, and pigs
2. Poultry
3. Tomatoes, oranges, pineapples, mangoes, pawpaw, and avocado
4. Onions, tubers, beans, carrots, and potatoes
5. Cotton seeds, peanuts, coconut, palm oil, and soy beans
6. Corn, sorghum, and millet
7. Rice
8. Yams and cassava
9. Cotton
10. Cocoa
11. Wool
12. Clay
13. Glass and sand
14. Gold
15. Limestone/gypsum
16. Iron ore
17. Salt
18. Marble
19. Bauxite

Kenya

Located in eastern Africa, Kenya was once ruled by the Arabs and the Portuguese, who came to trade for spices and slaves. Kenya was a British colony from 1895 until 1963, when it gained its independence. Today, Kenya is famous for the tremendous variety of its wildlife. The country's game preserves and parks attract tourists from around the world. Although much of Kenya consists of dry plains, farms in the highland region near the center of the country produce large crops of coffee and tea. Kenya's capital, Nairobi, is located in the highland. Rain forests, sandy beaches, and barrier reefs can be found along Kenya's scenic Indian Ocean coast. The city of Mombasa is Kenya's major seaport. Included among the more than 40 ethnic groups that live in Kenya are the Kikuyu, Kalenjin, Kamba, Luhya, Luo, and Masai. Some Kenyans, like the Masai, are nomads who herd livestock from one grazing place to another. But most Kenyans are farmers who either till a small piece of land or work on the large plantations. Since many Kenyans have large families, the country's population has been increasing at a rapid rate.

After Kenya gained its independence from Great Britain, this person was elected Kenya's first president in 1964. What was his name?

INVESTIGATIONS

What is the name of Kenya's largest ethnic group?

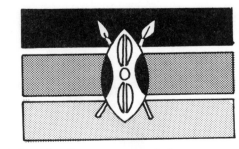

What do the stripes and the spears and shield on Kenya's flag symbolize?

Art: Students can make a colorful Kenya "quilt" to decorate the classroom bulletin board or wall. First, each student chooses one Kenyan scene or symbol to depict on a blank sheet of white paper. Let them draw, paint, color, or use markers. They can decorate their work with small pieces of fabric, yarn, string, ribbon, and other things which can be glued to the paper. The sheets of paper with the completed work can then be taped together to form the quilt. (Note: Instead of paper, squares of white cloth can be used.) Make certain students incorporate a variety of scenes and symbols into the design of the quilt. Here are some possibilities: the spears and shield from Kenya's flag; Kenya's coat of arms; the red, green, and black national colors; Kenya's motto, the Swahili word, *harambee*, which means "pulling together"; pictures of Kenya's famous wildlife including zebras, lions, elephants, rhinos, and giraffes; scenes of the Kenyan countryside which show its coastal plains and highland regions; and portraits of Kenya's ethnic groups such as the Kikuyu and Masai.

Geography: Challenge students to answer the following questions about Kenya's geography: What countries and bodies of water border Kenya? (Sudan, Ethiopia, Somalia, Tanzania, Uganda, and the Indian Ocean) What are the nation's major rivers? (Athi and Tana) What are the country's major lakes? (Turkana and Victoria) What is Kenya's capital? (Nairobi) and What is the nation's highest point? (Mt. Kenya, 17,058 feet).

Paleontology: The area of anthropology that deals with early human and prehuman remains is called *human paleontology*. Paleontologist Louis Leakey has found evidence of early humans in the Great Rift Valley, which runs through Kenya. The fossil bones and teeth he has excavated suggest that humans lived on earth two million years ago, and that Africa might be the birthplace of the human species. Have interested students find out more about the Leakey family and their amazing discoveries.

Writing: As a creative writing lesson, give each student the name of one of Kenya's wild animals. Tell them that they are to imagine that they are wild animal photographers sent to Kenya to track down and photograph their assigned animals. After students have researched their animals, they can write creative stories about their adventures. Encourage them to include colorful details and to make the stories as exciting as possible. They can illustrate their stories with photographs or drawings of their animals.

Cartography: Making a large-size map of Kenya on posterboard is a great way for students to sharpen their geographic skills. Let small groups of three or four students decide which type of map they want to make. For example, some may want to make a map of Kenya's game parks, or another group may want to show Kenya's physical features. Make certain that students include scales, legends, and compass roses on their maps.

Kenyan Historical Happenings

Like many African countries, Kenya's history is about its people's struggle to regain their freedom and independence after hundreds of years of foreign domination. Below are listed five headings which describe important periods in Kenya's history. Use library resources to find out about each period. Then write a short paragraph on the lines provided that tells about each one.

1. The Early History of Arab and Portuguese Control of Kenya

   _____

   _____

   _____

2. The Period of British Colonial Rule

   _____

   _____

   _____

3. The Struggle for Independence

   _____

   _____

   _____

4. Kenya Gains Independence

   _____

   _____

   _____

5. Building a New Nation

   _____

   _____

   _____

Name _____

Kenya Word Search

Use your research skills to answer the questions below about Kenya. Then find the words in the puzzle. These words can be found horizontally, vertically, diagonally, or backwards. Circle the word.

Clues for Word Search

1. _____ Africa's tallest mountain across the border
2. _____ The main economic activity
3. _____ The main tourist attraction
4. _____ The first president of Kenya
5. _____ The main region where coffee is grown
6. _____ The Swahili word that means "pulling together"
7. _____ Kenya's largest lake
8. _____ The national language
9. _____ Borders Kenya on the northeast
10. _____ The capital city
11. _____ Tall animal found in Kenya.
12. _____ This geographic line runs through the center of Kenya.
13. _____ Kenya's official language
14. _____ Kenya's colonial ruler
15. _____ Kenyan movement that opposed British
16. _____ Eastern Kenya faces this ocean.
17. _____ Kenya's chief cash crop
18. _____ Kenya's biggest national park
19. _____ A tall slender group of nomads
20. _____ What corn is called in Kenya
21. _____ They visited Kenyan coast 2,000 years ago.
22. _____ One of Kenya's chief rivers

```
U X C D A W A I L A M O S M O W T Q S X C V M A K B L
V W E L I I I H E S Q A W V N J Q Q J V R V K L G V V
A P Q F S P G Q I I D N A L H G I H W K K J P G K A R
T E A E X X U H N H W S H W U L H U M X N B M M H R G
T O H H K A P C D Z T K I S H O G W H J U O G Q P D K
A O G A T Y G X I U M B L L Y J L G W H D Z P Q S Q P
Y I B O R I A N A H V P I J F K I V T Y N M O G S B N
N A R R C A O K N G I H S G Q M A U M A U M S E C I U
E G B Z C V M X M C A J S C B T U R K A N A I R R R Y
K R R E A O X B M F X R E I W Q E G Z F T A E A E O Q
W I L D L I F E E J B J Y V L H S J Z Q B J P I S H C
F C L E R N Q F S E N N G F V G M H H L M S A N F A I
V U Y I V R O W E J S C B S S E N P M A I E L N G I M
W L N O M A E U M E G I L N C V P E R X D L Y Z A Y T
I T M R P A Z N T L B I L D I B T B X Q G B Y B S T T
S U X X D T N G A F J I R N G Q I M K M H Q Q P R M K
I R T P L Q U J T U D J S A I N M J K E P O H A I N H
P E Z L V B I X A J S K B P F T T S D C U Q F J H P O
N Z G O C D G X G R Z R A C W F N A A I Z B B G A O P
A U M J K K F P M C O T R N O Y E P B L Y R N J M U Q
K H W V M E U X U C N U A J N N L G N J L I S K U T S
X J B T C S H F N Z W Z F C B Z X G A Q E T M Y E Z S
A J N V Q Y H B C C F Z X L T V I M K Q O A R P G B E
H K A T K B R Q J M U D D D T H G N P Q X I I B G Q N A
D X J N V E M E H P R G Y U Q L R Y K Z B N N D B H T
Q J A Y K Z B M U T I G I G I T K P E O H E Z I V L F
```

Zambia

Zambia is a landlocked country slightly bigger than Texas located in South Central Africa. Although Zambia is in the tropics, it lies on a high plateau, which gives the country a moderate climate. Hundreds of years ago the Bantu people moved into the area. It is their descendents that inhabit Zambia today. Most of the people live in the capital, Lusaka, or in cities in a region known as the Copperbelt, which is located along the Zaire border. As the name of the region suggests, copper is a big part of Zambia's economy. In fact, it is the nation's most important mineral and chief export. However, for many years now the world price for copper has dropped steadily. This has prompted the government to look elsewhere for income. One promising source is tourism. The unspoiled nature of Zambia is probably its most important resource. Rich in scenery and wildlife, Zambia has many national parks, including South Luangwa National Park, which some claim is the finest wildlife sanctuary in Africa, if not the world. The park is teeming with thousands of elephants, hippopotamuses, and buffalo.

INVESTIGATIONS

Zambia is a landlocked country. What nations border Zambia?

Zambia's open pit mines like this make the country one of the world's largest producers of a very useful mineral. What is this mineral which is Zambia's most important export?

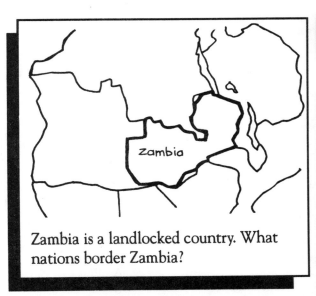

Zambia's most popular tourist attraction is a world-famous waterfall named for a British queen. What is the fall's name?

Curriculum Connections

Economics: Copper is the mainstay of Zambia's economy. The Copperbelt in north-central Zambia has the most concentrated copper mining complex in the world. Since copper is Zambia's main export, world supply and demand for the metal are crucial to the country's future. Let interested students research the following topics related to the economics of copper. Make a list of all the products that are made with copper components (the list should be extensive). Make a list of products originally made from copper that are now made from some other material (the list might include examples like pipes and tubing, which are now often plastic). List Zambia's major export markets (the list will demonstrate that Zambia's major markets are industrialized countries such as Japan, Italy, France, and Britain). Calculate how far these export markets are from Zambia (the calculations will show the great distances between Zambia and its major markets). List Zambia's major competitors for the copper market (the list will include more developed countries like Chile and the United States, which also have large deposits of copper ore).

Government: In 1991 Zambia moved from one-party, one-person rule to multi-party, democratic government. Reforms are currently underway to restore personal liberties and human rights. In the 1980s the old government proved unable to deal with either falling world prices for copper which ruined Zambia's economy or the severe famine caused by drought. Have students research Zambia's natural and human resources and then make a list of recommendations for the new government on ways it can improve the country's prospects for the future.

Science: Thousands of visitors are attracted to Zambia's game parks each year for safaris. Have groups of three or four students create "Wild and Wonderful Vacation Tour Guide" books that accurately describe the characteristics, behaviors, and habitats of Zambia's wildlife. Students can illustrate their guide books with colorful pictures or drawings.

Mathematics: Zambia has an estimated population of 8,073,000. Forty-three percent of this population lives in urban areas. Have students calculate how many Zambians live in urban and rural areas. The current growth rate of Zambia is estimated at 3.7 percent a year. Ask students to make the following calculation: If the rate of growth continued at 3.7 percent a year, how many years would it take Zambia's population to double? (The answer is 19 years.)

Geography: Zambia is a landlocked country. Let students use physical maps of southern Africa to determine the most likely routes goods and people might travel to reach the Indian Ocean from Zambia. Then let them compare their predictions with actual transportation routes shown on appropriate maps of the countries in the region found in encyclopedias and atlases.

Name _____

Zambian Customs and Courtesies

In any country or culture there are traditional customs and courtesies that the local people follow. This is especially true of the rural areas. If you visited Zambia, it would be helpful to know some of the traditional customs described below. On the right side on the page, explain how Zambian customs in certain situations compare to American customs in the same situations.

Zambian Custom   **American Custom**

1. **Visiting:** Unannounced visitors at mealtime are expected to share host's food.

2. **Eating:** The fingers of the right hand are used for eating. Men eat in a separate place from women and children.

3. **Care of Elderly:** The elders are shown great respect. Care of the elderly is the responsibility of the family.

4. **The Family:** The family is often large (six or seven children). Children's uncles and aunts are considered "fathers" and "mothers."

5. **Dating and Marriage:** Girls marry early, usually without dating first.

6. **Gestures:** It is disrespectful to point a finger at someone.

7. **Greetings:** Kneeling down before an elder or chief is common

8. **Attitudes:** Most Zambians are very patient and take life as it comes.

9. **Recreation:** Dancing is the main form of entertainment.

10. **Time:** People are flexible about time.

Name _____

Zambia Tourist Map

Because much of Zambia's environment is unspoiled, Zambia prides itself on being "The Real Africa." Below is an outline of a tourist map of Zambia. Missing from the map are the names and locations of Zambia's major tourist attractions, which are Zambia's 19 national parks. Use a map of Zambia to find the locations of the 19 parks listed below. Then plot them on the map. Use the number corresponding to the park's name to indicate its location on the map.

Zambia's National Parks

1. South Luangwa
2. North Luangwa
3. Lukusuzi
4. Luambe
5. Mweru Wantipa
6. Sumbu
7. Lusenga Plain
8. Isangano
9. Lavushi Manda
10. Kasanka

11. Kafue
12. Nyika Plateau
13. Lochinvar
14. West Lunga
15. Liuwa Plain
16. Siona Ngwezi
17. Mosi-oa-Tunya
18. Blue Lagoon
19. Lower Zambezi

LUSAKA ⭐

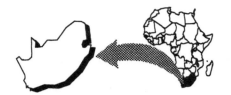

South Africa

South Africa is a nation rich in natural resources. It is the world's largest producer of diamonds, gold, and chrome. Besides mining, South Africa has well developed steel, tire, motor, textile, and plastic industries. South Africa's climate is similar to California's, and many areas are ideal for farming. Among the country's chief agricultural products are corn, wheat, sugarcane, tobacco, citrus fruit, and livestock. South Africa is noted for its spectacular scenery and great variety of wildlife. But the nation's political situation has kept many tourists away. The ruling white minority's policy of *apartheid*, which has forced the black majority population to live like "second-class citizens," has left the country in turmoil. South Africa is moving from apartheid toward freedom for everyone based on multiracial representative government. In 1993 a black South African, Nelson Mandela, and a white South African, F. W. de Klerk, shared a joint Nobel Peace Prize for their efforts to dismantle apartheid. Hopefully, South Africans will be able to reason together, and Africa's richest nation will take its place in the world community.

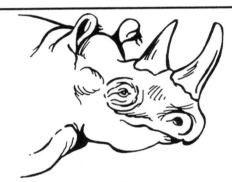

Large colonies of lion, elephant, leopard, cheetah, and rhino roam freely in South Africa's largest wildlife preserve. What is the name of the preserve?

INVESTIGATIONS

What world-renowned black leader has worked tirelessly to bring peace, prosperity, and freedom to all South Africans?

South Africa's largest city, Johannesburg, was founded because it was near one of the country's most valuable resources. What is the resource?

Curriculum Connections

Music: You can bring the "sound" of South Africa to your students by exposing them to some of the country's popular and indigenous music. Afro-rock, played by artists such as Johnny Clegg and his group Savuka, has been gaining international attention. Probably no one has done more to bring the vibrant, rhythmic music of the black South African townships to American listeners than Paul Simon with his highly successful album *Graceland*. Despite the album's "American" lyrics, the sound is distinctly South African and includes the choir music of Ladysmith Black Mambazo and Stimela.

Science: South Africa's mineral wealth is considerable. More than 50 minerals are produced in the country. Assign interested students the task of reporting on the following scarce and indispensable metals of which South Africa is the world's leading supplier: chromium, gold, manganese, platinum, and vanadium. South Africa is also a leading producer of diamonds, which is another mineral some students might want to investigate. Have students include information about the following topics in their reports: characteristics of the mineral, where the mineral is found, how the mineral is processed, and what the mineral's uses are.

History: The discovery of gold had a significant effect on the histories of both the United States and South Africa. Have students compare the California Gold Rush of 1849 with South Africa's gold boom of 1886. Specifically, students can compare the following: where the gold deposits were located, how the gold was mined, who mined for gold and who got rich, how the discovery of gold affected the people and society, why the discovery of gold was important, and when (if ever) the mining of gold stopped.

Sociology: South Africa is comprised of a number of ethnic groups. They include Zulu, Xhosa, North Sotho, South Sotho, Tswana, Shangaan-Tsonga, Swazi, Southern Ndebele, Northern Ndebele, and Venda. Each of these groups has its own language, culture, and traditional territory. The Zulu, which is the largest group, once had an independent kingdom under the rule of a powerful king named Shaka. Let students research the culture of Zulu or one of the other ethnic groups in South Africa.

Geography: Have students plan a trip that will take them to each of the following South African destinations: Johannesburg, Cape Town, Port Elizabeth, Durban, Kruger National Park, Transvaal Highveld, and Kimberly. As they plan their itineraries, make certain students research the attractions at each place. Let students also develop a list of clothing to take on the trip. When would be the best time to travel to South Africa? Will the fact that seasons are reversed in the Southern Hemisphere affect their choices regarding when to go and what clothing to take?

Name _____

This Is South Africa

Important South African people, places, and events are described in the left-hand column. Their names are listed in the right-hand column. Use research materials to match the pairs correctly. Place the correct letter on the blank in front of each numbered description.

_____ 1. This mineral was discovered in 1867.

_____ 2. An official language of South Africa

_____ 3. The legislative capital

_____ 4. Performed the world's first heart transplant

_____ 5. In 1990 this black African leader was released from prison.

_____ 6. In 1974 South Africa lost the right to participate in this organization.

_____ 7. Rich deposits of this mineral were discovered in 1886.

_____ 8. The first European country to reach South Africa

_____ 9. This country ruled South Africa for almost 150 years.

_____ 10. By 1825 this black African kingdom was the most powerful in southern Africa.

_____ 11. This war ended in 1902.

_____ 12. He won the 1984 Nobel Peace Prize.

_____ 13. South Africa's largest city

_____ 14. South Africa's policy of racial segregation

_____ 15. South Africa's largest wildlife park

_____ 16. Great Zulu king

A. The Netherlands
B. gold
C. Zulu
D. Kruger
E. Desmond Tutu
F. Johannesburg
G. apartheid
H. Boer
I. Shaka
J. Cape Town
K. Christian Barnard
L. Afrikaans
M. diamonds
N. Nelson Mandela
O. Portugal
P. United Nations

Name _____

Black South African Leaders

At the moment, South Africa is trying to move from the racism of apartheid toward a democratic and prosperous multiracial society. Three black Africans leading the march are Nelson Mandela, Desmond Tutu, and Mangosuthu Buthelezi. After you research these leaders, write a short biography on each of them in the space provided. What ideas does each leader have for solving South Africa's problems?

1. Nelson Mandela

_____
_____
_____
_____
_____

2. Desmond Tutu

_____
_____
_____
_____
_____

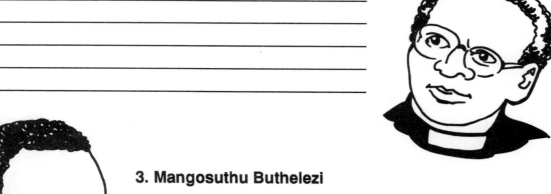

3. Mangosuthu Buthelezi

_____
_____
_____
_____
_____

Latin America:

An Overview for the Teacher

Latin America stretches from the Rio Grande in the north to Cape Horn in the south. It also includes the islands of the Caribbean. Altogether, Latin America covers an area of nearly eight million square miles. Almost all of Latin America was settled by either the Spanish or the Portuguese, and their descendants predominate in many of the countries of the region today. Spanish is the official language of most Latin American countries, and Portuguese is the official language of Brazil. Both of these languages developed from Latin, hence the name "Latin America."

Make a transparency of the political outline map of Latin America on the next page. Ask students to describe the shape of Latin America. Let students identify various countries and geographic features on the transparency. Encourage students to share any information they have about the various countries and cultures. Point out to students that Latin America includes a portion of North America (Mexico and the countries of Central America) as well as the continent of South America. Locate the equator on the map. Point out that while all of Latin America is in the Western Hemisphere, part of the region is in the Northern Hemisphere and part in the Southern Hemisphere. Also point out that portions of Venezuela, Colombia, Ecuador, Peru, Guyana, Suriname, French Guiana, Brazil, Mexico, and Central America are tropical, while Chile, Argentina, Uruguay, and Paraguay are temperate like the United States. Show students the location of the Andes Mountains, which dominate much of the geography of the western part of South America, and the Amazon River Basin, which is the location of the world's largest tropical forest.

Latin America is a land of great contrasts. There are lush tropical forests and arid deserts, soaring mountains and flat pampas, crowded cities and empty wilderness, beautiful cathedrals and ugly slums, abundant natural resources and scarce investment capital, rich and poor.

Latin America is predominately a developing area with economic characteristics very different from those of the United States. The region has been slow to develop for a number of reasons. During the period of European colonization, economic activity centered on extracting valuable minerals and growing a few plantation crops for export. Today, there is still too much dependence in many Latin American countries on one or two export products. Other problems include unemployment, low productivity, inequality, a lack of technical skills, and incompetent governments.

The United States and Latin America have much in common. Both were European colonies, both struggling for independence, and both are part of the "New World." The United States itself is becoming increasingly "Latin." Hispanics are one of the fastest growing segments of the U.S. population. The fifth largest Spanish-speaking country in the world is the United States.

UNITED STATES

MEXICO

Gulf of
Mexico

Mexico City

CUBA

BELIZE

GUATEMALA
Guatemala City

HONDURAS
Tegucigalpa

EL SALVADOR
Managua

NICARAGUA

COSTA RICA
San Jose

PANAMA
Panama City

Caracas

VENEZUELA

Georgetown

GUYANA
Paramaribo
Cayenne
SURINAME
FRENCH
GUIANA

COLOMBIA
Bogata

Quito

ECUADOR

PERU

BRAZIL

Lima

Brazilia

BOLIVIA
Sucre

Pacific Ocean

PARAGUAY

Asuncion

Atlantic Ocean

CHILE

ARGENTINA

URUGUAY

Santiago

Buenos Aires

ideo

Latin America

FS-10124 Countries and Cultures

Mexico

Almost three times the size of Texas, Mexico is located in southern North America. Mexico is the United States' closest Latin American neighbor. The two countries share a common border that stretches from the Pacific Ocean to the Gulf of Mexico. Mexico and the United States are friends and major trading partners. This was not always the case, however. In 1848 Mexico was forced by the United States to give up much of what is now the U.S. Southwest, including California. Mexico has a long and rich history. The ruins of the Mayan and Aztec temples stand as examples of some of the greatest feats of engineering in the ancient world. In the early 1500s the Aztec empire was destroyed by the Spaniards. Today, Mexico's capital, Mexico City, rests on the site of the Aztec capital, which was called Tenochtitlan. With a population of over 20 million, Mexico City is the world's largest city. Mexico's major industries include food, tobacco, chemicals, oil, coffee, and cotton. Tourism is also important to the country's economy.

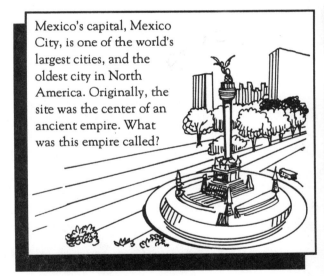

Mexico's capital, Mexico City, is one of the world's largest cities, and the oldest city in North America. Originally, the site was the center of an ancient empire. What was this empire called?

INVESTIGATIONS

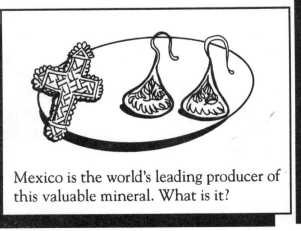

Mexico is the world's leading producer of this valuable mineral. What is it?

This person became the president of Mexico in 1988. What is his name?

Curriculum Connections

Art: Mexican mural art is world famous. Many Mexican painters used the Mexican Revolution of 1910 as a theme for their mural art. Show students examples of the mural art of Jose Orozco, Diego Rivera, and David Siqueiros found in art books and other resources in the school or community library. Ask students to discuss what kind of mood or feeling these artists were trying to evoke in their paintings. Encourage interested students to report on one of the artists.

Music: Play an audio tape of Mexican folk and popular music. (The music or Spanish teacher may be able to help you locate some authentic Mexican music.) Mexico is well-known for its *mariachis* bands. These strolling musical groups include singers and trumpet, violin, and guitar players. Music and dancing are an important part of Mexican festivals or *fiestas*. One of the most exciting and colorful folk dances is the Mexican hat dance. Show students a photograph, or better yet a videotape, of Mexican folk dancing.

Geography: Challenge students to use their mapping skills to find Mexican cities. Give students the latitude and longitude of the following Mexican cities, and then let them find them: Mexico City (19°N latitude, 99°W longitude), Guadalajara (20°N latitude, 103°W longitude), and Monterrey (25°N latitude, 100°W longitude). Encourage students to gather latitudes and longitudes of other Mexican cities and quiz one another on their locations.

History: Have students use encyclopedias and other library resources to create a time line that includes the following important dates and events in Mexico's history: mid-1300s–Aztecs found Tenochtitlan, 1519-1521–Hernando Cortés conquered Aztecs, 1821–Mexico gained independence, 1824–Mexico became a republic, 1848–the United States defeated Mexico in the Mexican War, 1910-1911–Mexican Revolution, 1938–Mexico nationalized the oil industry, 1970s–huge oil deposits were discovered, 1985–earthquakes in central Mexico killed over 7,000, and 1993–North American Free Trade Agreement (NAFTA) between the United States, Canada, and Mexico was ratified.

Culture: Have students investigate Mexican food, clothing, and customs. Students would probably enjoy sampling bite-sized pieces of some traditional Mexican foods such as *tortillas, enchiladas, tacos,* and *tostadas*. Is Mexican-style food served in the school's cafeteria? Let students research traditional Mexican clothing, which includes such items as colorful *ponchos, serapes,* and *sombreros*. Among Mexico's important holidays are the following: Independence Days (September 15 and 16); Guadalupe Day (December 12), which is the country's most important religious holiday; and Christmas, which is when Mexican children play the piñata game. In the game the children try to break open an animal-shaped clay or paper figure, called a piñata, filled with candy and toys. Have the students make papier-mache piñatas for display in the classroom.

Name _____

Mexican Matchup

Use your research skills to match these people, places, and things to learn some facts about Mexico. Put the letters on the right on the blanks by the proper numbers on the left.

_____ 1. A major language spoken in Mexico

_____ 2. A word used in the United States that comes from Mexico

_____ 3. This country invaded Mexico.

_____ 4. The main Mexican food made from corn

_____ 5. The most popular spectator sport in Mexico

_____ 6. During the Christmas holidays, this is filled with candy.

_____ 7. Mexican dictator

_____ 8. Mexico's most valuable natural resource

_____ 9. Where many Mayan ruins are located

_____10. Mexican revolutionary leader

_____11. Separates Texas and Mexico

_____12. Mexico faces this body of water on the west.

_____13. Mexico's largest land region

_____14. The large estates of wealthy land owners

_____15. They destroyed the Aztec empire.

_____16. Mexico is the world's leading producer of this mineral.

_____17. Mexico is a part of this continent.

_____18. A famous Mexican painter

A. Porfirio Diaz
B. Emiliano Zapata
C. oil
D. David Siqueiros
E. Rio Grande
F. Mayan
G. piñata
H. tortilla
I. Plateau of Mexico
J. Yucatan Peninsula
K. Pacific Ocean
L. France
M. bullfighting
N. canyon
O. silver
P. Spaniards
Q. North America
R. haciendas

The Aztec-Chocolate Connection

The ancient Aztecs of Mexico introduced the world to chocolate. The passage below is about the Aztec-chocolate connection. Some facts are missing from the passage, however. Your job is to use encyclopedias and other library resources to find the missing facts. Write the correct facts on the appropriate blank spaces. After you complete the passage, list 15 food items that contain chocolate on the spaces at the bottom of the page.

According to Aztec legend, chocolate was a gift of the _____ (1). The Aztec god _____ (2) brought the _____ (3) to the Aztecs. The Aztecs believed that if they ate chocolate, they would gain _____ (4). The Aztecs also liked to make a _____ (5) from ground chocolate. Only _____ (6) Aztecs could afford chocolate often. Chocolate is made from the _____ (7) bean. Chocolate was so _____ (8) that the Aztecs used the beans for _____ (9). The Aztecs were growing the beans before the _____ (10) arrived in _____ (11). _____ (12), who conquered the Aztecs, took some beans to _____(13). It became very popular on the continent of _____(14). Eventually, chocolate spread around the world, and now there are choco-late-lovers everywhere. Among the leading _____ (15) bean growing countries today is _____ (16).

List 15 foods that contain chocolate:

_____   _____   _____

_____   _____   _____

_____   _____   _____

_____   _____   _____

_____   _____   _____

Guatemala

Some 2,000 years ago, Guatemala was the center of the remarkable Mayan culture. The Mayans built impressive cities, and they were highly skilled in mathematics, astronomy, and the arts. Guatemala is land of diverse geography. There are towering mountains, including 33 volcanoes, lush rain forests, crystal clear lakes and rivers, and beaches on the Pacific and Caribbean coasts. About half of the country's over nine million inhabitants are descendants of the ancient Mayans. Their life today is much as it was with their Mayan ancestors. They live in villages and grow small plots of vegetables, including the basic staple of their diet, corn. Some of Guatemala's chief products for export are coffee, cotton, sugar, and bananas. Guatemala City is the nation's capital as well as the center of commercial activities. Guatemala has been racked with social and political turmoil. One source of conflict is the unequal distribution of land. A few rich people in Guatemala control most of the country's land, while the vast majority are landless and poor. After years of military rule, a civilian government gained control of Guatemala in 1986.

What is the name of this traditional Guatemalan musical instrument?

INVESTIGATIONS

The ruins of the ancient city of Tikal were discovered in Guatemala's tropical rain forest. Who built Tikal?

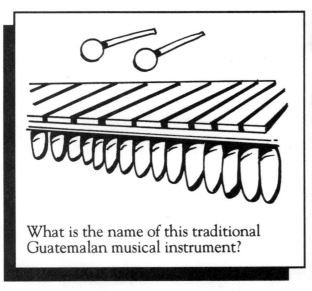

What is the name of the national bird of Guatemala which is displayed on the country's coat of arms?

Curriculum Connections

Mathematics: Like most countries around the world, Guatemala uses the metric system. Have students use the scale on a map of Guatemala to calculate the distances in kilometers between Guatemala City and the following Guatemalan cities: Flores (488 kilometers), Tikal (548 kilometers), Quezaltenango (206 kilometers), and Coban (528 kilometers).

Art: Because of their colorful and intricate designs, clothing and cloth bracelets woven in Guatemala are very popular in the United States. Try to locate examples of Guatemalan textiles to show students. Guatemalans today weave cloth with looms that are almost identical to those used by the ancient Mayans. Using Guatemalan motifs as guides, students can use strips of colored construction paper to weave their own place mats with Guatemalan-style designs. Display the students' completed place mats on the wall.

Geography: Have students use maps found in encyclopedias, atlases, and other sources to locate information about the major geographic features of Guatemala. They can identify major cities, rivers, lakes, mountains, vegetation, and bordering countries and bodies of water. Students can trace a map of Guatemala on posterboard and draw symbols to represent the geographic features.

Archeology: In conjunction with the student activity "Mayan Civilization," students can use library resources to write reports about one of the following aspects of Mayan culture: religion, family life, food, clothing and shelter, trade and transportation, government, education, language and writing, or arts and crafts. Encourage students to illustrate their written reports with drawings and pictures depicting the Mayan way of life.

Science: Agriculture is Guatemala's most important industry. Assign students the task of reporting on the various steps in the production of one of the country's chief crops. They are as follows: coffee, bananas, cotton, sugar, cardamom, and corn.

Current Events: Over the years Guatemala's large population has been plagued by poor government, warfare, earthquakes, and poverty. Have students gather news information on Guatemala from newspapers, magazines, television, and radio. Does the plight of people in Guatemala seem to be getting better or worse? Based on the information they have collected, let students give oral news reports on recent events in Guatemala.

Language Arts: Have students write a paragraph designed to promote tourism to Guatemala. Encourage students to include vivid language and colorful details to get their readers interested.

Guatemalan Culture

The passage below describes the Guatemalan people. Some of the facts are missing, however. Your job is to find the correct facts and then write them on the blank spaces. Consult library resources to make certain you get the facts right.

Guatemalan society consists of two basic groups, the Indians and the Ladinos. Indians are descendants of the _____ (1). They speak an _____ (2) language, although the majority of Indians also speak Spanish. The typical Indian family lives in small _____ (3). Males usually work in the _____ (4) while the females take care of the _____ (5). Everyone is involved with the hand crafting of embroidered_____ (6) and meticulously carved _____ (7). The basic diet staple is _____ (8). It is easy to determine an Indian's home village by his or her _____ (9). The other major group, the Ladinos, or _____ (10), are usually of mixed Indian and _____ (11) ancestry. They usually live in the large _____ (12) and _____ (13). They speak _____ (14). Most of the Guatemalan people are members of the _____ (15) religion. Along with Christian rites, many Indians also practice ancient _____ (16) to help ensure a good harvest.

Mayan Civilization

The ancient civilization of the Maya was centered in Guatemala. The greatest Mayan city was called Tikal. Today, tourists can visit Tikal National Park and explore the temples and plazas. Some of the oldest buildings in Tikal date back to the third century B.C. Mayan accomplishments in the fields of mathematics, astronomy, and the measurement of time were astonishing. The Mayans also developed a hieroglyphic script (or written language) which has made it possible for people today to study and understand their history. The archeological sites that have been discovered at Tikal are shown on the map below. They include Temple of the Great Jaguar (A), Northern Acropolis (B), Temple of the High Priest Jaguar (C), and Temple of the Two-Headed Serpent (D). Use library resources to find out more about Tikal. Specifically, on a separate sheet of paper, answer these questions:

1. Who lived in Tikal? Who lived near Tikal?

2. Who ruled Tikal?

3. What was the religion of the Mayans like?

4. What were some of the main occupations of the Mayans at Tikal?

5. How did the Mayans build Tikal?

6. Why did the Mayan civilization vanish?

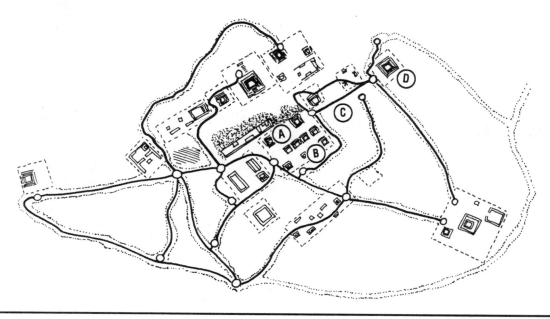

Costa Rica

Slightly smaller than West Virginia, Costa Rica is Central America's most peaceful nation. The country has no formal military organization. Costa Rica means "rich coast," and the country is trying to live up to its name. Its main exports are coffee, bananas, textiles, and sugar. But probably Costa Rica's most important asset is the ecological diversity of its rain forests, which attract scientists from throughout the world. Tourists also are discovering the breathtaking beauty of this tropical paradise, which seems to have something for everyone—beaches, fishing, river-rafting, horseback riding, rain forests, volcanos, wildlife reserves, national parks. Costa Rica has very good health and education systems. In fact, the nation's literacy rate is the highest in the region. Recently, Costa Rica has experienced tough economic times, but the government is attempting to create new industries and jobs, which should help raise the standard of living.

INVESTIGATIONS

Tiny Costa Rica has more species of butterflies and moths than the entire continent of Africa! What is Costa Rica's land area in square miles?

What do the stars on Costa Rica's coat of arms represent?

What past president of Costa Rica won a Nobel Peace Prize for his role in creating a regional peace plan for Central America?

Ecology: John M. Hamilton, in his recent book about the United States and the Third World, entitled *Entangling Alliances* (published by Seven Locks Press, located in Cabin John, Maryland), discusses Costa Rica's tropical rain forests in considerable detail. He points out that Costa Rican forests have more biological diversity per square foot than any other place on earth. He also states that Costa Rica has one of the best conservation programs in the world. Hamilton uses numerous examples to show that the value of plants in tropical rain forests is increasing rapidly because new uses for their genetic material are being discovered by scientists all the time. Have students research the connection between their own lives and the fruits, fibers, and medicinals from tropical plants in third world rain forests like Costa Rica's or Brazil's. To get students thinking about the connections, you may want to read them sections from Hamilton's or some other appropriate book. For more on the rain forest, read the other ideas on this page.

Community Action: Students who want to take an active role in saving the global environment can start by reading *50 Simple Things You Can Do to Save the Earth* (published by The Earthworks Press, located in Berkeley, California). This book is full of practical things your students can do to help protect the earth, including tropical rain forests. You and your students can also obtain information about the rain forests and what you can do by writing to Rainforest Action Network, 300 Broadway, Suite 28, San Francisco, CA 94133, or calling (415) 398-4404.

Science: Challenge small groups of three or four students to develop sets of recommendations for protecting the earth's tropical rain forests. Before the groups make their recommendations, they should gather as much information as they can on the topic. Perhaps there are global-environment experts in the community who would be willing to share their knowledge with the class. Students can also consult ecologically oriented magazines such as *World Monitor, Sierra, Wilderness,* and *Audubon,* which can be found in the school or community library. Related issues that students may want to examine include deforestation, soil erosion, climate change, and world demand for rain forest plant, animal, and mineral resources. Let a spokesperson from each group report to the class on the set of recommendations. Are the groups' recommendations similar or different from one another?

Language Arts: Encourage students in each of the groups (the groups are described in the activity above) to write a letter from their group addressed to each of their representatives in the U.S. Congress. The content of each group's letter should include the group's recommendations for protecting the earth's rain forests. The letter should also include a request for information about the representative's position on the topic.

Costa Rica Travel Brochure

Create copy for a travel brochure on Costa Rica. The brochure should contain interesting information that promotes Costa Rica as the perfect place for a family vacation. Use your research skills to investigate each of the topics below. Then write a short paragraph in the space provided that brings the topic to life and sparks interest in vacationing in Costa Rica. Finish the stages of creating an attractive brochure on a separate sheet of paper.

Costa Rica's national parks and reserves have some of the most spectacular scenery in the world.

_____
_____
_____
_____
_____
_____

Water activities in Costa Rica can be extremely enjoyable.

_____
_____
_____
_____
_____

Costa Rica's capital city, San José, has many interesting attractions.

_____
_____
_____
_____
_____

No other place in the world offers such a variety of plants and animals in such a small area.

_____
_____
_____
_____
_____
_____

Going Places in Costa Rica

Since Costa Rica is a small country, its attractions are only a short scenic drive from one another. If your family were traveling by car in Costa Rica, you would want to know the meaning of the traffic regulation signs below, which are in Spanish, found along the highways and streets. Match the signs with the English translations of the regulations on the right. (Hint: If you don't know Spanish, try to find someone who does to help you.) Write the appropriate letter on the blank space under the sign.

_____1. NO VEHICULOS AUTOMOTORES

_____2. ANCHO MAXIMO 18 m

_____3. NO ESTACIONAR

_____4. VELOCIDAD MAXIMA 60 KPH

_____5. PARADA DE TAXIS

_____6. NO ADELANTAR

_____7. PEATONES POR LA IZQUIERDA

_____8. SILENCIO

_____9. ALTURA MAXIMA 3 m

_____10. NO VIRAR EN U

_____11. SE PERMITE VIRAR EN U

_____12. MANTENGA SU DERECHA

_____13. ESTACIONA MIENTO UNA HORA 6 AM 6 PM

_____14. CEDA EL PASO

_____15. ALTO

A. No U-Turn

B. Maximum Width

C   Stop

D. Silence

E. Maximum Height

F. Stay Right

G. No Cars

H. U-Turn Permitted

I. Speed Limit

J. Yield

K. Taxi Stop

L. One-Hour Parking

M. No Passing

N. No Parking

O. Pedestrians to Left

Peru

Located on the western coast of South America, Peru was once the center of the ancient Inca empire. The Incas believed that their ruler was a descendant of the Sun-god and that they were the "children of the sun." From the remains they left behind, it is known that the Incas built highways and cities, created pottery and tapestries, crafted ornate objects of pure gold, and practiced medicine, including surgery. But since the Incas never developed a system of writing, there is no written record of their civilization for study. The Spanish, who arrived in 1532, conquered Peru and destroyed the Inca empire. In 1821 Jose de San Martin and Simon Bolivar freed Peru from Spanish control. Today, Peru's government is struggling with severe economic problems and with a terrorist group, called "Shining Path," which is trying to take over the country. Peru's major industries include mining, oil, fishing, and timber. Wheat, potatoes, beans, rice, coffee, and corn are among the chief agricultural products.

This animal is used to transport goods in Peru's rugged highlands. What is its name?

INVESTIGATIONS

The ancestors of Peru's Indians created a great empire which included the ancient city of Machu Picchu shown here. What were these people called?

This large snake found in tropical parts of South America, including Peru, crushes its prey by coiling around it. What is its name?

Curriculum Connections

Culture: Almost 50 percent of Peru's population is Indian and about 37 percent are Mestizos, or mixed Indian and white ancestry. Peru's Quechua Indians can trace their lineage back to the days of the great Inca empire. In fact, Quechua, the language of the Incas, is an official language of modern-day Peru. The Quechua Indians live in the mountains of Peru where they farm and raise livestock. The Indians who inhabit the Peruvian Andes have maintained many customs and traditions from pre-Inca times. Other Indian groups, like the Piro, Campa, and Machiguenga, live in jungle clearings in eastern Peru. Most of Peru's Mestizo population is concentrated in urban areas in Peru's coastal region. Assign students the task of investigating the Quechua or one of the many other Peruvian Indian groups. Specifically, students can report on the following aspects of the Indian group's way of life: housing, food, recreation, formal and informal education, religion, and types of work.

Geography: Geographic factors have had a significant effect on biological and physical processes in Peru. The cold Humboldt current which flows off the coast of Peru helped create a desert along the Peruvian coast because it prevented the creation of water vapor. But thanks to the Humboldt, the Pacific Ocean's temperature off Peru's coast is unusually mild for a hot, tropical region. The coastal water is also enriched by a continuous supply of organic material from Peru's rivers which originate in the Andes Mountains. The combination of mild temperature and rich organic material has created an ideal environment for tiny forms of marine life. And the marine life, in turn, provides a rich food source for a tremendous fish population. The abundant marine life also provides food for birds who leave their droppings on the coastal islands. The white droppings, called *guano*, are gathered and used as agricultural fertilizer. Fishing is one of Peru's major industries, and fish meal, which is made from dried sardines, is exported to countries throughout the world where it is used to feed livestock. Have students investigate how geographical factors have affected Peru's coastal region.

Science: The mighty Amazon River begins in the Andes Mountains of Northern Peru. Challenge students to gather scientific facts about the Amazon River Basin region for inclusion in a publication students can create entitled *The Amazing Amazon River Trivia Book*. Make certain students can document sources for the facts they collect. The source for each fact should be listed in the back of the publication. They can use encyclopedias, atlases, almanacs, magazines, and other sources to research the topic. To spark interest in the assignment, tell students the following facts from *The World Book Encyclopedia*: The Amazon River carries more water than any other river. The first European to see the Amazon was probably Vincente Pinzon. The Amazon river contains about 3,000 species of fish.

Peru's Geography

Peru has a population of over 22 million. Predict Peru's most important cities by indicating their locations on the small map of Peru below. After you have made your predictions, find the following geographic features on a map of Peru in an encyclopedia or atlas, and then draw them on the large outline map of Peru below.

1. The three distinct geographic regions:
   (a) Coastal Lowlands
   (b) Andean Highlands
   (c) Jungle

2. Peru's capital and other major cities

3. The Panamerican Highway

4. The Pacific Ocean

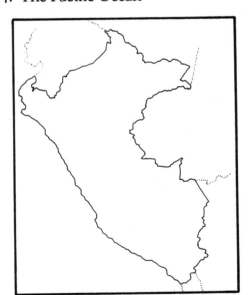

How close were your predictions to the actual locations?

Name _____

Peru From Top to Bottom

Listed below are the elevations of some of Peru's most important cities. Use the information to complete the bar graph showing elevation for each place. The letters on the graph correspond to the places listed below.

City	Elevation in Feet
a. Trujillo	131
b. Piura	82
c. Ica	1,326
d. Lima	502
e. Arequipa	7,800
f. Huaraz	10,036
g. Cusco	10,904
h. Machu Picchu	7,544
i. Puno	12,552
j. Pucallpa	505

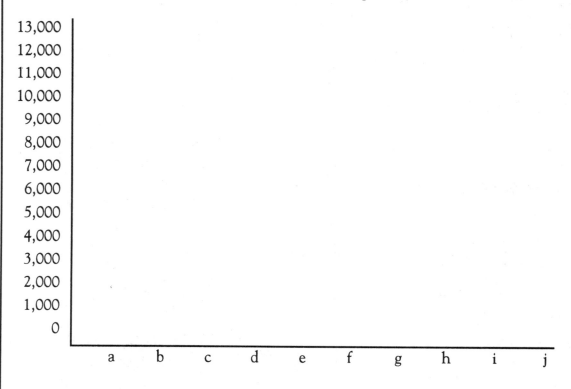

Elevation for Peru's Important Cities

Chile

Shaped like a stringbean, Chile is 2,650 miles long, but its average width is only 100 miles. Chile faces the Pacific Ocean to the west and the Andes Mountains to the east. Chile is divided into the following three regions north to south: the Northern Desert, the Central Valley and the Archipelago. Chile has rich mineral deposits in the Northern Desert. Huge amounts of copper and nitrates are found there. The Central Valley is the most populated region. It is where most of Chile's agriculture, industry, and commerce are situated. Chile's capital and largest city, Santiago, is located in this region. The chief crops grown on the fertile plains north and south of Santiago are grain, onions, beans, potatoes, grapes, and other fruit. The region also has deposits of copper, iron ore, coal, and manganese. Forests cover much of the region to the south. Very few people live in the cold, rugged Archipelago region. For many years the Chilean people were ruled by dictators, but since 1990 a democratically elected government has been in power.

INVESTIGATIONS

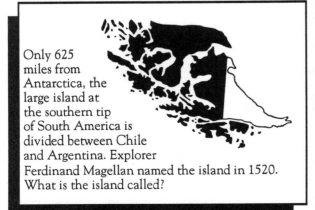

What is the name of the island possession of Chile in the South Pacific that is famous for its mysterious stone statues?

Only 625 miles from Antarctica, the large island at the southern tip of South America is divided between Chile and Argentina. Explorer Ferdinand Magellan named the island in 1520. What is the island called?

This is one of the many churches in Chile's beautiful capital city. What is the name of the capital?

Curriculum Connections

Geography: Students can test one another on Chile's geography by constructing true-false quizzes. First, let students use library resources to generate a list of 10 true or false statements on Chile's geography. Then, after the statements have been checked for accuracy, have students exchange quizzes so that no one has his or her own quiz. Next, let students use library resources to determine if the statements on the quizzes are true or false. After students complete the quizzes and check their answers, have them hand in the quizzes to you. You can use the true-false statements to play the following game, which is a fun way to review and practice the material learned. Randomly divide the class into two teams. To start the game, read one of the statements from one of the quizzes and call on one student from one of the teams to tell you if the statement is true or false. Repeat the process with a student from the other team and continue taking turns until all of the students on both teams have had an opportunity to participate. Each time a student answers correctly, that student's team gets one point.

Language Arts: Challenge students to generate a list of adjectives which accurately describe some aspect of Chile. For example, Chile could be described as "skinny" or "thin" because of its long, narrow shape or "rugged" because of its mountainous terrain. Collect the adjectives and check them for accuracy. Then rearrange the letters of the adjectives and give the students a list of the scrambled adjectives to unscramble. After students have unscrambled the adjectives, ask them to use the adjectives in sentences about Chile.

Science: Chile's exports consist mainly of copper, molybdenum, and iron ore. Assign students the task of researching one of these important minerals. Specifically, ask students to report on the particular mineral's properties, how the mineral is formed, where the mineral is found in Chile, how the mineral is mined, how the mineral is separated from ore, and what types of products are made from the mineral.

Art: Have each student create a large collage which reflects the richness of Chile's land and people. They can use pictures cut from magazines as well as drawings and paintings they have made. Also let them include words or phrases related to Chile cut from newspapers and magazines. The completed collage should be a colorful and accurate representation of Chile's society, economy, geography, and history.

Mathematics: Chile's total number of employed workers is 4,112,200. What percentage of the total is each of the following top four economic activities? Services (1,305,700 workers), Manufacturing (640,300), Trade (706,400), and Agriculture (823,300).

Name _____

Chilean Economic Profile

How many people live in Chile? What do they do? Where do they live? Answering the questions below will help you better understand Chile's economy. Use a current encyclopedia or world almanac to do this exercise.

1. What is Chile's population? _____

2. Compared to the other South American countries, what is Chile's rank
   in population? _____

3. What is Chile's land area in square miles? _____

4. Chile has approximately four million employed workers. What percentage of Chile's
   population is employed? _____

5. What are Chile's major industries?

   _____

   _____

   _____

   _____

6. List three of Chile's chief crops?

   _____

   _____

   _____

7. What are Chile's two main exports?

   _____

   _____

8. Many of Chile's employment opportunities are in urban areas. What are Chile's four
   largest cities. What is each one's population?

   _____

   _____

   _____

   _____

Name _____

Chile's Liberator

Bernardo O'Higgins was a hero in Chile's war for independence against Spain, and he was Chile's first president. But some of O'Higgins' actions angered his supporters. The words listed below are associated with O'Higgins' character and life. Use the words from the list and what you learn about O'Higgins from library resources to write a paragraph describing his life.

courageous	reformer	San Martin
arrogant	liberal	1818
defiant	fighter	Maipo River

_____
_____
_____
_____
_____
_____
_____
_____
_____
_____
_____

Brazil

Brazil is a melting pot of races and cultures. First colonized by the Portuguese, Brazilians are descendants of Europeans, Africans, and Indians. Brazilians have an immense country to call home. The largest country in Latin America, Brazil is a land of awesome beauty–the vast Brazilian rain forest, the mighty waters of the Amazon, the thundering Iguacu Falls, as well as a sandy coastline lapped by the waters of the Atlantic Ocean. Brazil is also a land of sharp contrasts. It is a highly productive country. With a rich natural endowment and human resources, Brazil is a leading producer of cars, airplanes, chemicals, electrical equipment, sugar, coffee, meat, forest products, and minerals. But Brazil is also burdened with many problems. Among them are the destruction of the rain forest for timber and agriculture, overcrowding and slums in the cities, and widespread unemployment. In 1992 delegates from 178 countries came to Rio de Janeiro to attend the Earth Summit, where saving the Amazon rain forest was one of the most important topics.

INVESTIGATIONS

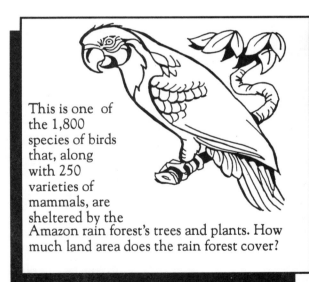

This is one of the 1,800 species of birds that, along with 250 varieties of mammals, are sheltered by the Amazon rain forest's trees and plants. How much land area does the rain forest cover?

There are many distinctive buildings found in Brazil's capital city. What is the capital of Brazil?

Corcovado Peak and this famous 130-foot statue, which stands on its 2,329-foot summit, are symbols of Rio de Janeiro. What is the name of the statue?

Ecology: The Brazilian government is attempting a very difficult ecological balancing act. On the one hand, the nation has accepted responsibility for the preservation of the Amazon rain forest environment. Toward that end, it has enacted policies to protect tracts of forested land in the Amazon Basin, which is the location of the world's largest tropical forest. On the other hand, Brazil wants to exploit the rain forest's tremendous economic potential. Have students research the following questions: Are there ways to use the resources of the rain forest without destroying the trees? Would uses that sustain the forest provide more or less revenue than cutting timber and clearing the land?

Language Arts: One use of the rain forest encouraged by the Brazilian government is ecological tourism. In 1989 the Amazon region was visited by about 170,000 tourists, of which 70 percent came to Brazil. The Organization of American States (OAS) estimates that international tourism in the Amazon region may grow 12 percent to 15 percent per year over the next five years. Challenge small groups of three or four students to create travel brochures that would attract foreign tourists to the Brazilian Amazon. The brochures should include interesting information and colorful illustrations about Amazon rain forest attractions. Students can consult library sources for ideas about information and pictures for inclusion in their brochures.

Art: Students can use ballpoint fabric paints to decorate old, white T-shirts (brought from home) with Brazilian sights and symbols. For example, students might choose to decorate their shirts with pictures of tropical animals and plants native to Brazil, or they might want to depict scenes from the Amazon rain forest and Rio de Janeiro's famous ocean front, or they might want to paint the Brazilian flag on their shirts. As an alternative activity, let individuals or small groups of students decorate assigned sections of a large sheet with Brazilian scenes. When completed, the decorated sheet can be displayed on the wall of the classroom. The ballpoint fabric paints are available at craft and sewing stores.

Geography: Provide students with an outline map of Brazil. Let them use encyclopedias and atlases to identify and locate on a map the nine Brazilian metropolitan areas which have populations of over one million. Students can then plot and label the metropolitan areas on their outline maps. The nine areas are São Paulo, Rio de Janeiro, Belo Horizonte, Salvador, Fortaleza, Curitiba, Recife, Porto Alegre, and Belem.

Culture: Have students investigate and report on important cultural aspects of the following Brazilian holidays: New Year (January 1), Martyr of the Independence (April 21), Labor Day (May 1), Independence Day (September 7), Proclamation of the Republic (November 15), Christmas (December 25), Mardi Gras (date changes), Corpus Christi (date changes), and Good Friday (date changes).

Dateline Brazil

Important dates in Brazil's history are listed below. Match the event to the year(s) it happened by putting the letter inside the box next to the date on the timeline. Use library resources to help you match the dates and events.

Events

A. First coffee plants smuggled into Brazil

B. Amazon rubber boom

C. The colonial capital was moved to Rio de Janeiro.

D. Magellan stopped briefly at Rio de Janeiro.

E. Dutch captured Brazil's colonial capital, Salvador

F. Portugal's king was forced into Brazilian exile by Napoleon.

G. The new capital of Brasilia was built.

H. The first of three million African slaves were brought to Brazil.

I. Brazil declared its independence from Portugal.

J. Gold was discovered in Brazil.

K. French force captured Rio de Janeiro

L. President Midici was inaugurated.

M. Pedro Alvares Cabral accidentally discovered Brazil.

N. Brazil's slaves are freed.

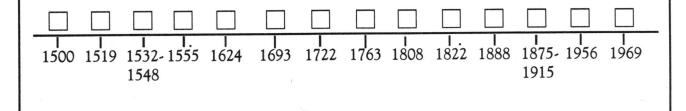

1500 1519 1532- 1555 1624 1693 1722 1763 1808 1822 1888 1875- 1956 1969
             1548   1915

Brazil's Geography

Brazil is divided into 22 states. Some of Brazil's states are listed below on the right. On the left are clues about these states. Use library resources to help you match the clues with the places. Write the letter on the blank space.

Clue

_____ 1. Belém, in the mouth of the Amazon, is here.

_____ 2. The only major city here is Macapá.

_____ 3. Its name means "dense forest."

_____ 4. Salvador is its capital city.

_____ 5. Manaus, a city first made rich by rubber, is found here.

_____ 6. Brazil's southernmost port is here.

_____ 7. The industrial center of Brazil is located here.

_____ 8. First rich in gold, and now rich in iron ore

_____ 9. The art and fashion center of Brazil

_____ 10. Brasilia is surrounded by this state.

_____ 11. Fortaleza, an old city on the coast, is here.

_____ 12. Maceió is the capital of this state.

_____ 13. Recife, known as the "Brazilian Venice" is here.

State

A. Mato Grosso
B. Bahia
C. Sao Paulo
D. Rio Grande de Sol
F. Amazonas
G. Goiás
H. Para
I. Rio de Janiero
J. Ceará
K. Minas Gerais
L. Pernambuco
M. Alagoas
N. Amapá

Argentina

After Argentina's great general, Jose de San Martin, defeated Spain in 1816, Argentina became an independent nation. Almost twice the size of Alaska, Argentina is the second largest country in South America. Stretching along Argentina's western border are the Andes Mountains, including Mount Aconcagua, the Western Hemisphere's highest peak (22,831 feet). In the middle of Argentina are fertile plains called *pampas*. Argentina is famous for its *gauchos,* or cowboys, who herd cattle on the pampas. Livestock are important to Argentina's economy, and the nation is a major meat exporter. Other chief farm products include wheat, corn, oilseed, and hides. Argentina's trade and commerce is centered in Buenos Aires, the capital and largest city. Located near the mouth of the Plata river, Buenos Aires' harbor is dotted with ships from around the world waiting to load and unload goods. Some of Argentina's most important industries are chemicals, textiles, and machinery. Argentina has a mild climate. Since the country is in the Southern Hemisphere, its seasons are opposite those of the United States.

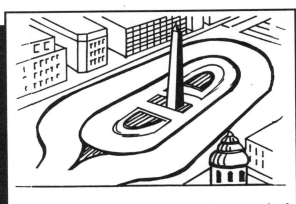

This magnificent plaza is in the capital of Argentina. What is the capital of Argentina?

INVESTIGATIONS

What are Argentine cowboys called?

What mountain range separates Argentina and Chile?

Social Studies: Like the United States, Argentina was once under colonial rule and had to fight to gain its independence. Have students write reports about the history of Argentina. They can use encyclopedias and other library resources to research the topic. The report should include a time line with important dates in Argentina's history. Encourage students to examine any significant similarities and differences between Argentine and U.S. history. They can include maps showing changes in Argentina's political boundaries over time. Tell them to also include in their reports news information about recent developments in Argentina found in newspapers and magazines and on television.

Geography: Six of Latin America's 10 highest mountains are located in or on the border of Argentina. Challenge students to find the names and locations of the six mountains. The six mountains from the highest to lowest are as follows: (1) Aconcagua, (2) Ojos del Salado, (3) Don Conos, (4) Tupungato, (5) Pissis, and (6) Mercedario.

Mathematics: Argentina is divided into 1 federal district, 22 provinces, and 1 territory. The largest province is Buenos Aires. Argentina's total area is 1,073,400 square miles. Have students calculate Argentina's population density by dividing Argentina's total population (32,700,000) by the total land area. Then have students calculate Buenos Aires' population density by dividing the province's total population (10,865,408) by the province's total land area (118,754). Let students compare the two population density figures. What inferences about Argentina's population can students draw from the comparison?

Language Arts: Have students create booklets entitled *The Basic Argentina Visitors' Guide*. The booklet should emphasize the tremendous diversity of Argentina's landscapes, from the rugged Andes Mountains in the west to the windswept terrain of Tierra del Fuego in the south. The booklets should also highlight information about places to go to see Argentina's natural and cultural attractions. The booklets can also include a chart containing information about Argentina's climate.

Biographies: Assign students the task of reporting on one of Argentina's notable personalities. Let them select an Argentine from among the following: Jorge Luis Borges, Luis M. Drago, Alberto Ginastera, Eva Duarte de Perón, Juan D. Perón, and Jose de San Martín.

Economics: Argentina's economy has suffered from severe inflation. Have interested students research this topic. Specifically, they can report on the causes of Argentina's high inflation rate and what is currently being done to reduce inflation.

Argentina's Land and People

Argentina's geography is diverse. Use a map of Argentina in an encyclopedia or atlas to find Argentina's four main land regions. The four regions are: (1) Northern Argentina, (2) the Pampa, (3) the Andine, and (4) the Patagonia. Next, use library resources to identify the geographic and cultural features from the list below that are characteristic of a particular region. Finally, write the appropriate features for each region in the space provided.

Northern Argentina: _____

_____

_____

The Pampa: _____

_____

_____

Andine: _____

_____

_____

Patagonia: _____

_____

_____

Gran Chaco	Colorado River	Tierra del Fuego
fertile plains	Andes Mountains	Piedmont
hard wood forests	poor soil	Mesopotamia
rolling plains	Mount Aconcagua	dry lakes
humid	Puna	summer floods
gaucho	skiing	

Argentine Crossword

Use your research skills to complete this crossword puzzle about Argentina.

Across
1. Farming region
4. Britain and Argentina fought over these islands.
6. Argentina was once this nation's colony.
9. Argentines of Indian and European ancestry
11. Symbol on Argentina's flag
12. Argentina's national beverage
13. Argentina's name comes from this mineral.
14. Chief export
15. Waterfall between Brazil and Argentina
16. Argentina lies this direction from equator
17. Capital of Argentina
18. Argentine cowboy

Down
1. Argentine leader
2. Argentina's main religion
3. Argentina's national dance
5. Southern Argentina region
7. About 600 miles south of Argentina
8. Argentina's hero
10. Large Argentine ranches
17. Shares Argentina's northern border

Uruguay

Located on the southeastern coast of South America, Uruguay is slightly smaller than Oklahoma. Uruguay struggled for its independence first from European powers, then from Brazil and Argentina, its two giant neighbors. Most of the country's population is of European background. The language and primary cultural influence is Spanish. The nation has some of the best farmland in South America. Among the chief crops are wheat, rice, and corn. Much of the land is ideally suited for grazing livestock. Many of Uruguay's main exports are agricultural products, including meat, wool, hides, and leather goods. Uruguay had one of the highest standards of living in South America, but Uruguay's economic development began to slow down in the late 1960s. In the 1970s the military took over the government. In the 1980s income from exports dropped abruptly. Today, democratic rule has been restored in Uruguay, and efforts to rebuild the economy are under way.

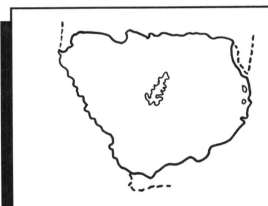

Uruguay is located between two giant neighbors. What are the names of the two countries?

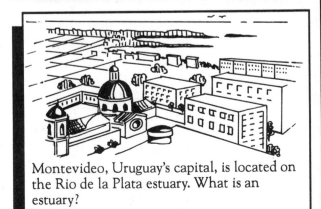

Montevideo, Uruguay's capital, is located on the Rio de la Plata estuary. What is an estuary?

INVESTIGATIONS

Though traditionally a cattle-raising country, Uruguay's number one export is not steers but another type of livestock. What is the largest export?

Curriculum Connections

Geography: Have students use a map or globe to find Uruguay's relative and absolute geographic location. Then ask students to write a brief paragraph in which Uruguay's geographic location is described. The students' paragraphs should include the following information: Uruguay is a triangular-shaped country located in South America. Uruguay is in both the Western and Southern Hemispheres. It borders Brazil on the north and northeast. It borders Argentina on the west. Its eastern shores are on the Atlantic Ocean. Uruguay lies 30 to 36 degrees south of the equator and between 53 and 58 degrees west of the prime meridian.

Economy: Agriculture and manufacturing are important parts of Uruguay's economy. Have students answer the following questions: What geographic factors make the land suitable for agriculture? (mild temperature, adequate rainfall, fertile land). How much of the land is suitable for agriculture? (90%). What are Uruguay's chief agricultural exports? (beef, wool, hides and leather goods, fish, and rice). What percentage of Uruguay's gross domestic product (GDP) is contributed by agriculture? (about 20%). What percentage of Uruguay's GDP is contributed by manufacturing? (23%). What are Uruguay's major industries? (meat processing, wool and hide preparation, sugar processing, textiles, footwear, leather apparel, tires, cement, fishing, oil refining, and wine production). In what ways does Uruguay's geography contribute to the nation's economic development?

Education: Uruguay's education is compulsory and free of charge. Religious instruction is not allowed in public schools. Uruguay's literacy rate is very high, 94 percent of the population over 10 years of age can read and write. A country with a high literacy rate frequently has a high standard of living. Have students use library resources to research Uruguay's standard of living. Have students gather information about Uruguay on the following standard of living indicators: child mortality, life expectancy, number of medical doctors and hospital beds, daily protein consumption and calorie intake per capita, gross domestic product per capita, and the availability of electricity. Based upon their analysis of the standard of living indicators, what generalizations can students make about Uruguay?

International Affairs: Uruguay is a member of the United Nations and most of its agencies. Have students research Uruguay's positions at the U.N. on such international issues as terrorism, pollution, nuclear proliferation, overpopulation, drugs, refugees, and global peacekeeping. The charter of the Alliance for Progress, an international program to promote economic and social development in Latin America, was signed by the United States and 19 Latin American countries on August 17, 1961, in Punta del Este, Uruguay. Have students research the program's history. Was the program successful?

Uruguay Trackdown

Use library resources to track down the answers to the following questions about Uruguay.

1. What is Uruguay's full name? _____

2. At what latitude and longitude is Montevideo located?

   _____

3. How much territory does Uruguay cover? _____

4. What is Uruguay's climate like? _____

   _____

5. Who is the national hero of Uruguay? _____

6. What is Uruguay's per capita Gross Domestic Product?

   _____

7. What is Uruguay's main crop? _____

8. What is Uruguay's main export? _____

9. What is Uruguay's population? _____

10. Name the official language of Uruguay. _____

11. Why is Uruguay's coastal area known as the "Riviera of South America"?

    _____

12. What is the name of Uruguay's international airport?

    _____

13. What are Uruguay's rolling hills and plains called?

    _____

14. What ethnic group makes up the largest part of Uruguay's population?

    _____

15. What are the names of Uruguay's two largest political parties?

    _____

Mapping Uruguay

Although a tiny nation, Uruguay is situated by giant neighbors. Use a map of Uruguay in an encyclopedia or atlas to find the geographic features listed below, and then label the features on the outline map of Uruguay.

Montevideo
Rio de Plata
Uruguay River
Brazil
Argentina
Atlantic Ocean
Cuchilla Grande
Coastal Plains
Lake Rincon de Bonete
Rio Negro

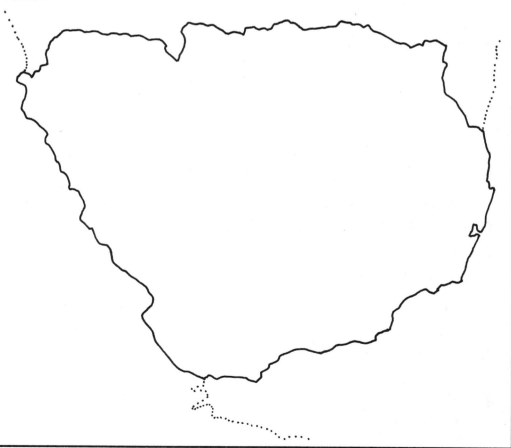

Northern America
An Overview for the Teacher

The United States and Canada have much in common. Both are former British colonies, basically English-speaking countries, important trading partners, and long-time friends, who share the world's longest undefended border. Because of their English roots, the two nations have been collectively referred to in the past as Anglo-America, but that term is becoming increasingly archaic. Both Canada and the United States are pluralistic societies with large minority populations. The United States has large African-American, Hispanic, and Asian minorities, which are growing, while Canada's French-speaking minority, which numbers over 25 percent of its population, maintains a distinct cultural identity.

Both Canada and the United States were settled about the same time. The British established their first permanent settlement in America at Jamestown in 1607. The French founded New France or Quebec in 1608. New France became a British colony in 1763. But nationhood came much sooner for America than for Canada. American colonists' grievances against the British culminated in 1775 at Lexington Green with the firing of the first shots of the Revolutionary War. During and after the war, thousands of English loyalists fled the American colonies for the Canadian Maritime Provinces and Ontario. In 1792, as Americans began the task of building a new nation, Britain created two provinces in colonial Canada. The two were French-speaking Lower Canada and English-speaking Upper Canada. This arrangement did not work and Canada was reunited in 1840. In 1867 Canada became an independent nation.

During the nineteenth century Canada's development lagged behind the United States' for a number of reasons. Although, like the United States, Canada had a wealth of natural resources, they were not as easily accessible. Canada's harsher environment and less suitable farmland inhibited westward migration across Canada. Unlike the United States, Canada had no indus-trialized east coast. For these as well as other reasons, about one million Canadians moved to the United States in the late 1800s.

In the twentieth century both Canada and the United States have developed strong economies and have assumed international responsibilities. Canada's commerce and industry rank among the top nations in the world. Seventy percent of Canada's trade is with the United States. Economic collaboration between the two countries continues to increase. The United States and Canada came to the aid of Europe during the two world wars. Like the United States, Canada is an active member of the United Nations, and it has supported U.N. peacekeeping operations.

Make a transparency of the political outline map of the United States and Canada on the next page. Invite students to identify various places on the map. Have students share any information they have about the two nations.

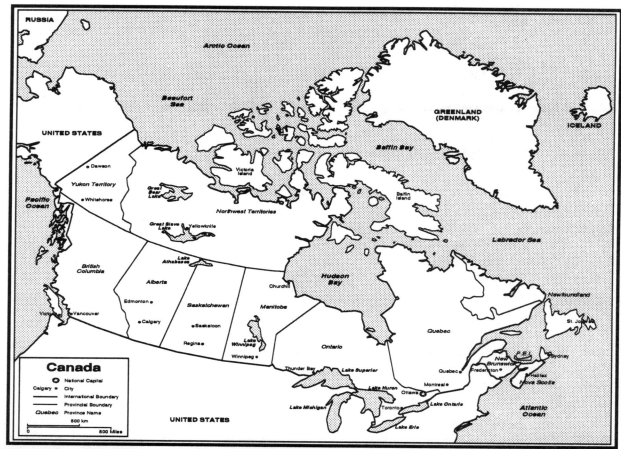

Canada

- ⊙ National Capital
- Calgary • City
- ——— International Boundary
- ——— Provincial Boundary
- Quebec Province Name

500 km
0
600 Miles

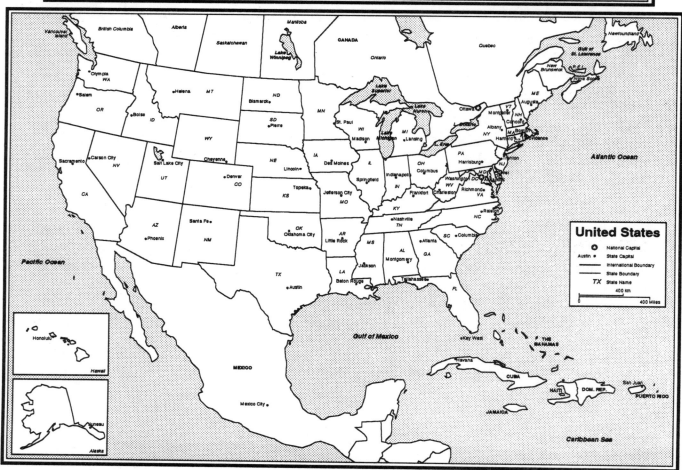

United States

- ⊙ National Capital
- Austin • State Capital
- ——— International Boundary
- ——— State Boundary
- TX State Name

400 km
0
400 Miles

United States of America

With the world's third largest population and fourth largest land area, the United States is a nation of tremendous geographic and cultural diversity. It is a land of spectacular natural wonders from icy glaciers in Alaska to fiery volcanoes in Hawaii to majestic canyons in Arizona to towering mountains in Wyoming. It is also a land of rich natural and human resources from oil fields in Texas to wheat fields in Kansas and from scientists in California to car makers in Michigan. The United States leads the world in the production of agricultural and industrial goods.

It is a rich mosaic of people from every corner of the world. Native Americans comprise almost one percent of the total population. Many Americans trace their cultural heritage to Europe. Other Americans' roots are in Africa, Latin America, the Middle East, and Asia. The values Americans share are what binds them together—values like freedom, justice, and equality. Despite the United States' great wealth, there are still some Americans who live in poverty, especially minority groups. Since the collapse of the Soviet Union and the end of the Cold War, the world has looked increasingly to the United States for leadership.

The faces of four of America's most famous presidents—Washington, Lincoln, Jefferson, and Theodore Roosevelt—are carved on Mt. Rushmore. In what state is Mt. Rushmore located?

INVESTIGATIONS

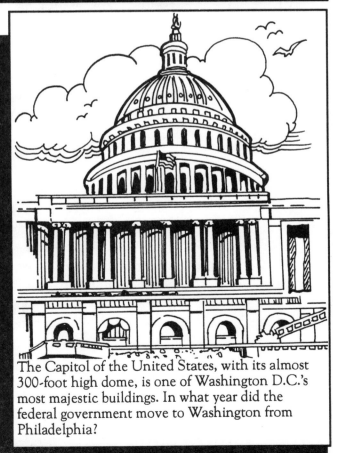

The Capitol of the United States, with its almost 300-foot high dome, is one of Washington D.C.'s most majestic buildings. In what year did the federal government move to Washington from Philadelphia?

The Great Seal of the United States was approved by Congress in 1782. What does the inscription *E pluribus unum* mean?

Art: Introduce students to a sampling of American folk art. Produced by both amateur and professional artisans, folk art, or "primitive," works are characterized by their simplicity and directness of statement. Show students various folk art paintings (found in art books from the school or community library or the art teacher). Ask them to discuss what the pictures reveal to them about "America." Include paintings by Thomas Hart Benton, John Steuart Curry, Grant Wood, and Grandma Moses. Encourage students to create their own folk painting of American scenes found in their own community.

Culture: Assign students the task of researching either the history of one native American tribe or the life of one famous native American. From A to Z, a list of tribes from which the students can choose follows: Algonkin, Arapaho, Arkansas, Blackfeet, Cherokee, Cheyenne, Chickasaw, Chippewa, Choctaws, Comanche, Creek, Crow, Delaware, Flatheads, Fox, Hopi, Hurons, Iroquois, Kansas, Kickapoo, Kiowas, Mandans, Miami, Mohawk, Narragansett, Natchez, Navaho, Nez Perce, Oneida, Osage, Ottawa, Paiutes, Pawnees, Pima, Potawatomi, Pueblo, Sauk, Seminoles, Senecas, Shawnee, Sioux, Snake, Utes, Winnebago, and Zuni. Students who want to report on a famous native American can choose one from the following list: Black Hawk, Cochise, Geronimo, Hiawatha, Pocahontas, Pontiac, Powhatan, Pope, Maquinna, Tecumseh, Sacajawea, Sequoyah, Chief Joseph, and Sitting Bull. Encourage students to illustrate their written reports with appropriate pictures of native American scenes.

Mathematics: Have students make a line graph entitled, "The Population of the United States from 1790 to 1990," using the population figures for various census years that follow: 1790 (3,929,214), 1810 (7,239,881), 1830 (12,866,020), 1850 (23,191,876), 1870 (39,818,449), 1890 (62,974,714), 1910 (91,972,266), 1930 (122,775,046), 1950 (150,697,361), 1970 (203,235,298), and 1990 (248,709,873). What inferences can students draw from the completed graph? Do they think the pattern of population growth will continue, or will it change in the future?

History: Challenge each student to select the top 10 most important events in American history. Have students make time lines to display their choices. After students have independently selected their 10 events, they can illustrate each one on a separate index card. Then students can hang the cards in chronological order from four-foot pieces of string. Let each student present his/her time line to the class. Each student should be prepared to explain the historical significance of each selected event. After all students have had an opportunity to make their presentations, see if the class can reach a consensus about the importance of any of the events on the time lines.

Name _____

State Flags

Each of the 50 U.S. state flags has features that make the flag unique. Key features of some of the state flags are listed below. Use your research skills to correctly match the feature on the flag with the state. Write the names of the states on the blank spaces.

_____ 1. a pelican

_____ 2. a buffalo

_____ 3. a shield and feathers

_____ 4. a bear

_____ 5. a ship

_____ 6. black and yellow diamonds

_____ 7. a red sun

_____ 8. a palm tree

_____ 9. an anchor

_____ 10. a big red C

_____ 11. a red cross on a white field

_____ 12. a dead tyrant

_____ 13. "United We Stand" "Divided We Fall"

_____ 14. "The Sunshine State"

_____ 15. "1848"

_____ 16. a green field

_____ 17. the Union Jack

_____ 18. the stars and bars

_____ 19. "Battle Born"

_____ 20. three white stars

_____ 21. a torch

_____ 22. "December 7, 1787"

_____ 23. The North Star and Dipper

Name _____

America's Multiethnic Society

The United States is one of the most ethnically diverse countries in the world. The pie graph below can help you see the ethnic composition of the United States. Use the pie graph to answer the questions below. Write your answers on the blank spaces provided.

Ethnic Composition of the United States

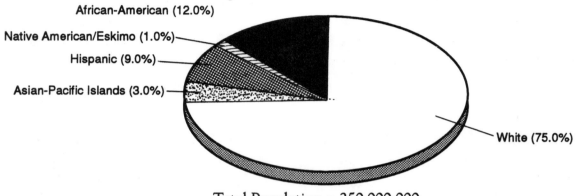

Total Population = 250,000,000

1. Which group accounts for the largest percentage of the total?
   _____

2. How many people are white?
   _____

3. Which group accounts for the smallest percentage of the total?
   _____

4. How many people are Hispanic? _____

5. How many people are African-Americans? _____

6. What group on the pie graph would include Latin Americans?
   _____

7. What group on the pie graph would include Chinese? _____

8. Use library sources to find out which ethnic group in the United States is growing at the fastest rate? _____

9. Based on the information displayed in the pie graph, on a separate sheet of paper write a paragraph describing the composition of the United States' multiethnic society.

Canada

Canada is the second largest nation in the world in area, but it has only 27 million inhabitants. The United States is almost nine times larger in population. The Vikings were the first Europeans to reach present-day Canada around A.D. 1000. The French established the first permanent settlement in Quebec in 1608. After the French and Indian Wars, the British gained control of Canada. In 1867 Canada became an independent nation. Most of Canada's people live in cities and towns along the country's southern border. On this ribbon of land are found farms, forests, mines, manufacturing centers, and major highways and railroads. Toronto is the largest city and an important inland ocean port. Canada is one of the world's most industrialized nations, and its citizens enjoy a high standard of living. The United States is Canada's major trading partner. Although basically an English-speaking country, Canada's French-speaking citizens number over 25 percent of the population. Most French Canadians live in the province of Quebec. Canada's second largest city, Montreal, has the distinction of being, after Paris, France, the largest French-speaking city in the world.

INVESTIGATIONS

These fishing boats will be sent out to sea from Canada's easternmost province. What is the name of this province?

What native American group lives in the Canadian Arctic?

Canada's national law enforcement officers with their wide-brimmed hats, scarlet coats, and heroic history are world-famous symbols of Canada. What is the official name of this group of officers?

Curriculum Connections

Culture: Cultural conflict between French- and English-speaking Canadians dates back to the eighteenth century. The French Canadian majority in Quebec has managed to hold on to its cultural identity, but it has felt threatened by the English-speaking majority in Canada as a whole. It is the English Canadians who have traditionally held Canada's economic and political power. The English-speaking population, in turn, is alarmed at French Canadian demands for more power and a separate French-speaking state. Assign students the task of debating one of the side's positions on the conflict. Before students debate, they should investigate the historical roots of the conflict and be knowledgeable of both sides of the issue.

Science: Canada has an abundance of mineral resources. Mining accounts for six percent of Canada's total gross domestic product, compared to two percent of the United States'. The two most important minerals are oil and natural gas. Canada's other major minerals include nickel, zinc, copper, gold, molybdenum, potash, and silver. Have students report on one of Canada's minerals. Specifically, they can report on where it is found, how it is mined, how it is processed, and what uses it has.

Art: Among Canada's native people, some, like the Haida on the Pacific coast, were excellent carvers. The Haida carved elaborate masks with movable parts that transformed the shape of the mask. For example, a mask with an outer carving in the shape of a hawk could open to reveal an inner carving of a human face. Show students pictures of native Canadian mask carvings. After they see some examples, students can make their own masks out of paper. They will need poster or cardboard, scissors, and wire to construct the masks. They can decorate the masks with paint or magic markers. Yarn, applied to the mask with glue, can be used to represent hair.

Geography: In general, Canadians seem to know a lot more about the geography of the United States than Americans seem to know about Canada's geography. Try the following activity to help students learn the names and locations of Canada's provinces and territories. Provide each student with a blank political outline map of Canada. (The names of the provinces and territories should be listed around the margins of the map.) Using the overhead projector, display the same map and place names on the screen. Slowly, one at a time, point to the name and location of each of the provinces and territories. Say the place name and point to its location. Signal for students to do the same thing. To enhance students' recall of the material, use some simple associations. For example, tell them to remember that Ontario is "*on* top of the Great Lakes," or that Saskatchewan is "too *skinny* to write its name across the province," or that Manitoba is in the "*middle* of Canada." To check for understanding, ask students to point to places on the map as you say them. If necessary, reteach.

Canada's Provinces and Territories

Canada is a federation comprised of 10 provinces and two territories. (The two territories are the Yukon and Northwest Territories.) The provinces and territories are listed on the right below. On the left are clues about them. Use library resources to help you correctly match the clues and provinces/territories. Write the letters on the blank spaces in front of the clues.

Clues

_____ 1. Leading producer of wheat

_____ 2. The Alaska Highway begins here

_____ 3. Directly north of the Great Lakes

_____ 4. Located in the Gulf of St. Lawrence

_____ 5. Location of Auyuittuq National Park

_____ 6. Whitehorse is the capital

_____ 7. Location of the *Golden Horseshoe*

_____ 8. The largest of the *Maritime Provinces*

_____ 9. Discovered by the Vikings

_____ 10. Home of the "Nordiques"

_____ 11. The largest of the *Prairie Provinces*

_____ 12. Floral emblem is the Pacific dogwood

_____ 13. Halifax is the capital

_____ 14. The smallest population

_____ 15. The largest population

_____ 16. Has Canada's mildest climate

_____ 17. Birthplace of Wayne Gretzky

_____ 18. Borders North Dakota and Minnesota

Provinces/Territories

A. Alberta
B. British Columbia
C. New Brunswick
D. Newfoundland
E. Nova Scotia
F. Manitoba
G. Ontario
H. Northwest Territories
I. Prince Edward Island
J. Yukon
K. Quebec
L. Saskatchewan

Name _____

Canadian Word Search

Use the clues below and library resources to complete this puzzle about Canada. Write the answers on the blank spaces provided. Then find the word in the puzzle. The words can be found vertically, horizontally, diagonally, and backwards. Circle the words.

Clues for Word Search

_____ 1. Canada's system of government
_____ 2. A major seaway (2 words)
_____ 3. Canada's busiest seaport
_____ 4. Canada leads the world in its production
_____ 5. Symbol on Canada's flag (2 words)
_____ 6. Canada's first Prime Minister
_____ 7. Canada's national holiday (2 words)
_____ 8. French Canadian motto, "I _____"
_____ 9. Major Canadian political party
_____ 10. "Canada" is an Indian word meaning _____.

_____ 11. Elected prime minister in 1968
_____ 12. Won Nobel Peace Prize in 1957
_____ 13. An official language of Canada
_____ 14. Canada's oldest city
_____ 15. Canada's capital
_____ 16. A major mineral product
_____ 17. National park in Alberta
_____ 18. A national symbol
_____ 19. Ethnic group of mixed French and Indian lineage
_____ 20. Canada's highest mountain

```
E  R  Q  T  R  U  D  E  A  U  L  A  A
A  W  A  T  T  O  N  I  C  K  E  L  B
D  L  A  N  O  D  C  A  M  S  U  S  E
E  C  N  E  R  W  A  L  T  S  E  F  A
J  S  L  W  R  E  V  U  O  C  N  A  V
A  I  O  S  L  A  R  E  B  I  L  E  E
S  T  G  P  H  S  I  L  G  N  E  L  R
P  E  A  R  S  O  N  Q  U  E  B  E  C
E  M  N  I  V  I  L  L  A  G  E  L  F
R  C  A  N  A  D  A  D  A  Y  L  P  G
Y  R  A  T  N  E  M  A  I  L  R  A  P
R  E  B  M  E  M  E  R  V  L  X  M  H
```

ANSWER KEY

Europe

Britain

Investigations   Page 3
1. The lion stands for England and the unicorn for Scotland. The harp on the shield stands for Ireland.
2. William Shakespeare
3. Big Ben

British Government   Page 5

1. C	8. M
2. L	9. C
3. C	10. M
4. M	11. C
5. C	12. M
6. L	13. L
7. M	14. L
	15. C

The Four Lands of Britain   Page 6

1. E	11. S
2. S	12. S
3. E	13. E
4. E	14. S
5. W	15. W
6. S	16. W
7. E	17. S
8. S	18. NI
9. NI	19 E
10. E	20. E

Germany

Investigations   Page 7
1. The Brandenburg Gate
2. Martin Luther
3. "children's garden"

Traveling Through Germany   Page 9

Comparing Germany and the United States   Page 10
1. Americans don't shake hands almost every time they meet.
2. Many buildings are made of wood.
3. In America dinner guests don't usually bring flowers for the host.
4. Much fewer sidewalk cafes
5. This varies, but many houses in U.S. cities and towns have a front yard.
6. U.S. students have about ten weeks of summer vacation.
7. Most U.S. school children write with a pencil or ballpoint pen.

8. Most American students don't learn a foreign language.
9. Most U.S. streets are wider and made of blacktop or concrete.
10. There are no medieval castles.
11. In most states the school year is approximately 180 days.

Sweden

Investigations   Page 11
1. Pippi Longstocking
2. Alfred Nobel
3. Vikings

Swedish Is Spoken Here   Page 13

1. C	11. Q
2. D	12. O
3. L	13. F
4. J	14. R
5. H	15. S
6. P	16. K
7. G	17. B
8. N	18. M
9. A	19. I
10. T	20. E

A Swedish Family's Budget   Page 14

1. 43%	6. $4,800
2. income tax	7. $1,600
3. car	8. $2,400
4. 5%	9. $320
5. income tax and housing	10. $3,200
	11. answers will vary

France

Investigations   Page 15
1. train a grande vitesse
2. Joan of Arc
3. Eiffel tower

A French Feast   Page 17

1. E	8. N
2. I	9. A
3. J	10. G
4. F	11. D
5. C	12. B
6. H	13. M
7. K	14. L

The French Revolution   Page 18
Answers will vary.

Greece

Investigations   Page 19
1. Parthenon
2. Olympia
3. Aegean Sea

The Gods of the Ancient Greeks — Page 21

1. R
2. S
3. K
4. P
5. N
6. J
7. L
8. M
9. B
10. O
11. E
12. G
13. F
14. D
15. C
16. Q
17. I
18. A
19. H

Greek Word Search — Page 22

1. Mediterranean
2. peninsula
3. democracy
4. bouzoukis
5. Salonika
6. Orthodox
7. moussaka
8. tobacco
9. Ottoman
10. Olympus
11. El Greco
12. drachma
13. Ithaca
14. Easter
15. Athens
16. olive
17. Crete
18. alpha
19. lyre
20. blue

Italy

Investigations — Page 23

1. Vatican City
2. the Pantheon
3. Venice

The Roman Empire — Page 25

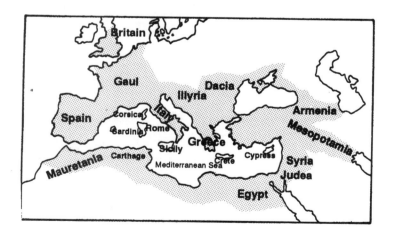

All About Italy — Page 26

(crossword solution)

Across/Down answers: TARANTO, GENOA, MUSSOLINI, ARIZONA, GLADIATORS, LIRA, PASTA, VIRGIL, CAESAR, GREEKS, ALPS, FIAT, ...

Russia

Investigations — Page 27

1. Leo Tolstoy
2. St. Basil's
3. St Petersburg, Peter the Great

The Birth of a New Russia — Page 29

1. President Gorbachev was overthrown.
2. Yeltsin called for general strike.
3. Demonstrators protested
4. Gorbachev reinstated as president
5. Gorbachev resigned as head of Communist Party.
6. Several republics declared their independence.
7. Soviet parliament voted to suspend the Communist Party.
8. Gorbachev proposed a new kind of Soviet Union.
9. Gorbachev resigned as Soviet president.
10. Soviet flag replaced by the flag of Russia

Russia's Czars — Page 30

1. Answers will vary, although responses should indicate an awareness that Peter's reign was less brutal and more constructive than Ivan's.
2. Answers will vary.
3. Answers will vary.

Spain

Investigations — Page 31

1. the flamenco
2. Miguel de Cervantes
3. Barcelona

Historic Spain — Page 33

1. E
2. J
3. H
4. M
5. O
6. Q
7. A
8. N
9. F
10. C
11. P
12. I
13. B
14. K
15. G
16. D
17. L

The Admiral of the Ocean — Page 34

Answers will vary.

The Orient

India

Investigations   Page 37
1. Mahatma Gandhi
2. Hinduism
3. Taj Mahal

Interesting India   Page 39

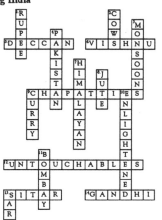

India's Many Languages   Page 40

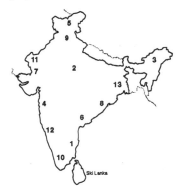

China

Investigations   Page 41
1. 4,000 miles
2. Confucius
3. Hong Kong

China's Long History   Page 43
1. Han
2. Buddhism
3. India
4. Marco Polo
5. Ming
6. Beijing
7. Manchus
8. Qing
9. European
10. Sun Yat-sen
11. Communist
12. Mao Zedong
13. Korean
14. Tibet
15. 1979
16. Tiananmen

Graphing China's Population   Page 44
1. increasing continuously
2. increase in birthrate, drop in infant mortality rate, and drop in death rate

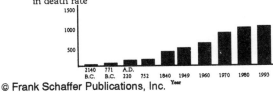

Japan

Investigations   Page 45
1. Honshu
2. Kimono
3. Shintoism

Japanese Festivals   Page 47
Answers will vary.

Japan's Urban Centers   Page 48

Korea

Investigations   Page 49
1. 1988
2. Buddhism
3. zither

Korea's Cultural Heritage   Page 51
1. A
2. B
3. C
4. D
5. D
6. C
7. B
8. A
9. C
10. D
11. B

Comparing South and North Korea   Page 52

	South Korea	North Korea
1. Land area	38,025 sq. mi	46,540 sq. mi.
2. Major cities	Seoul, Pusan Taegu, Inchon	Pyongyang
3. Population	43,134,000	21,814,000
4. Ethnic groups	Korean	Korean
5. Language(s)	Korean	Korean
6. Religion(s)	Shamanism, Buddhism, Confucianism, Christianity	
7. Government	Republic, Strong chief executive	Communist
8. Head of State	Pres. Roh Tae Woo	Pres Kim Il-Sung
9. Foreign policy	Pro-West	Anti-West
10. Per capita GNP	$5,600	$900
11. Chief crops	rice, barley, vegetables	corn, fruits, vegetables, rice
12. Natural resources	some coal, tungsten, graphite	coal, lead, tungsten, zinc, graphite
13. Major industries	electronics, ships, textiles, clothing, cars	textiles, petro-chemicals, chemicals, food processing
14. Chief exports	textiles, clothing, electrical mach., shoes, steel, cars	minerals, agricultural products

Thailand
Investigations — Page 53
1. rice
2. Bangkok
3. Buddhism

Buddhism in Thailand — page 55
1. Around 500 B.C., India, Buddha
2. To gain a state of peace and happiness called nirvana, the Noble Eightfold Path consists of the right understanding, thought, speech, action, livelihood, effort, mindfulness, and concentration.
3. Monks should live a life of poverty, meditation, and study.
4. Meditation involves discarding unwholesome thoughts, concentrating deeply, gaining a sense of calmness, and finally, achieving a state of pure awareness.

Colorful Thailand — Page 56
Answers will vary.

Indonesia
Investigations — Page 57
1. Mt Krakatau
2. Komodo Dragon
3. Garuda

Exotic Indonesia — Page 59
1. Found on Java, the one-horned rhinoceros is one of the most endangered and rare species in the world.
2. Found on Sumatra and Kalimantan
3. Found on Sulawesi, this animal resembles a wild boar
4. A rare bird found on Bali
5. Found on Sumatra and Kalimantan, this is Asia's only great ape.
6. Found on the island of Komodo, this is the world's largest living lizard.
7. Found on Sulawesi, this dwarf buffalo is the smallest of its species.
8. Beautifully plumed bird found on Irian Jaya
9. World's largest flower with blooms as big as three feet in diameter
10. A pungent-smelling fruit
11. A giant flightless bird found on Irian Jaya and Molucca

Indonesian Island Hopping — Page 60
1. C
2. E
3. G
4. C
5. B
6. B
7. A
8. B
9. G
10. F
11. B
12. D
13. B
14. E
15. G
16. C

The Pacific World
Australia
Investigations — Page 63
1. The large seven-pointed star represents the six states and territories of Australia. The other five small stars represent the constellation of the Southern Cross, which only can be seen in the Southern Hemisphere.
2. eucalyptus leaves
3. Sydney Opera House

Speaking Australian — Page 65
1. Q
2. L
3. K
4. P
5. M
6. O
7. N
8. A
9. B
10. U
11. S
12. H
13. D
14. T
15. R
16. I
17. C
18. F
19. G
20. J
21. V
22. E

Amazing Australia — Page 66
1. O
2. S
3. I
4. J
5. N
6. L
7. E
8. H
9. A
10. B
11. D
12. K
13. T
14. Q
15. R
16. C
17. P
18. F
19. G
20. M

New Zealand
Investigations — Page 67
1. Kiwi
2. Mt. Cook
3. Maori

Made in New Zealand — Page 69
1. farmer, rancher, lumberjack, miner, carpenter, food processor, fishermen, sheep shearer, dairy farmer
2. mining, agriculture, forestry, fishing, dairy
3. close proximity to water, pasture land, farm land, forests

New Zealand Cartography — Page 70
1. Taupo
2. Waikato
3. Wellington
4. Tasman
5. Waitangi
6. Cook
7. Stewart
8. North
9. South
10. Christchurch
11. Cook Strait
12. Southern Alps
13. Auckland

The Middle East
Kuwait
Investigations — Page 73
1. Persian Gulf
2. Iraq and Saudi Arabia
3. oil

Kuwait Scramble — Page 75
1. Kuwait City
2. barren
3. Palestinian
4. New Jersey
5. Iraq
6. dinars
7. Islam

An Arab Family in Kuwait — Page 76
1. Oldest male in the household is the head of the family. Traditionally, women serve the family, although increasingly women are participating in roles in business and the professions outside the home.
2. Islamic values influence the family's way of life.
3. Basic education is required and is free. The Islamic religion is taught in the schools
4. Foods made from wheat and other grains, eggs, vegetables, and fruits, including dates, are a main part of the diet. Most Arabs do not eat pork. Instead, chicken, lamb, and goat are eaten. Coffee and tea are popular drinks.
5. Loose-fitting clothing is worn. Many women wear garments that conceal their faces. Men wear traditional pieces of cloth on their heads.
6. Most Kuwaitis live in houses and apartments provided by the government.
7. Kuwaiti families in the cities have cars and trucks. In the rural areas, camels are still used.

Iran
Investigations — Page 77
1. Ayatollah Khomeini
2. Teheran
3. Darius

Iran Historical Happenings — Page 79
1. 1925
2. 1980-88
3. 550 B.C.
4. 1220
5. 1979
6. 1501
7. 331 B.C.
8. 1500s B.C.
9. 224
10. 1941
11. Mid-600s
12. 1906
13. 1794
14. 1989

Iran Crossword — Page 80

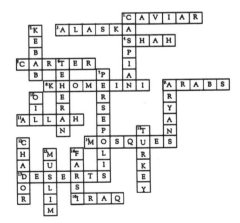

Iraq
Investigations — Page 81
1. Baghdad
2. Tigris and Euphrates
3. bazaars

Facts and Figures About Iraq — Page 83
1. Arabian
2. desert
3. fertile
4. rolling
5. mountainous
6. Euphrates
7. Tigris
8. Shatt-al-Arab
9. 169,235
10. 20
11. Baghdad
12. Arabs
13. Kurds
14. oil
15. dates, cotton
16. wool

Cradle of Civilization — Page 84
Answers will vary.

Saudi Arabia
Investigations — Page 85
1. Bedouins
2. mosques
3. "There is no god but God, and Muhammad is the messenger of God."

The Arabian Peninsula — Page 87
1. Bahrain
2. Saudi Arabia
3. Yemen
4. Kuwait
5. Riyadh
6. United Arab Emirates
7. Oman
8. Qatar
9. Mecca

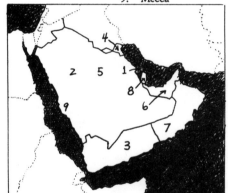

The Five Pillars of Islam — Page 88
1. Muslims must recite the creed "There is no god but God, and Muhammad is the Messenger of God."
2. Muslims must turn toward Mecca to offer prayers at dawn, noon, mid-afternoon, sunset, and evening. Although it is permissible to pray alone at home, it is recommended that Muslims pray in a Mosque, especially on Friday.
3. Muslims are obliged to give a percentage of their wealth for the welfare of the community and its neediest members.
4. Fasting is required during the holy month of Ramadan. The fast, which takes place between dawn and sunset, is considered an act of deep personal worship and also an exercise in self-control.
5. For Muslims who are able to make the journey, a pilgrimage to Mecca is the most significant expression of their faith.

Israel
Investigations — Page 89
1. Shield of David
2. Jimmy Carter
3. menorah, Hebrew language

Israel Word Puzzle — Page 91
1. democracy
2. kosher
3. Jerusalem
4. knesset
5. Tel Aviv
6. coastal plain
7. potash
8. kibbutzim
9. Jordan
10. Yom Kippur

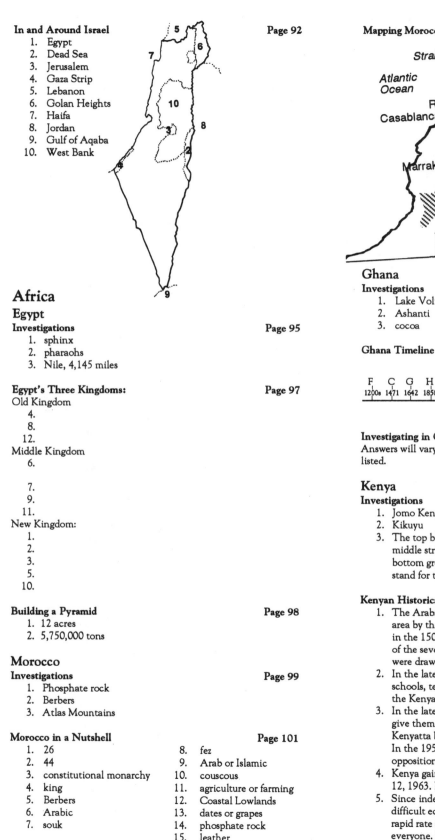

Africa
Egypt

Morocco

Ghana

F	C	G	H	K	D	J	L	A	E	I	B	M	N
1200s	1471	1642	1850s	1860s	1872	1886	1900s	1957	1960	1964	1966	1969	1972

Answers will vary, but all should reflect consideration of the factors listed.

Kenya
1. Jomo Kenyatta
2. Kikuyu
3. The top black stripe represents the Kenyan people, the red middle stripe their struggle for independence, and the bottom green stripe is for agriculture. The shield and spears stand for the defense of freedom

1. The Arabs arrived in Kenya first and were in control of the area by the eighth century A.D. The Portuguese took control in the 1500s, but the Arabs regained control toward the end of the seventeenth century. Both the Arabs and Portuguese were drawn to Kenya by the spice and slave trade.
2. In the late 1800s Britain gained control of Kenya. They built schools, tea plantations, and railroads, but they did not let the Kenyans control their own government.
3. In the late 1940s Kenyans started to demand that the British give them more political and economic rights. Jomo Kenyatta became the leader of the opposition to the British. In the 1950s fighting between the British and the Kenyan opposition, called the Mau Mau, occurred often.
4. Kenya gained its independence from Britain on December 12, 1963. Kenyatta became prime minister.
5. Since independence, Kenya has had to deal with a variety of difficult economic problems. The population is growing at a rapid rate and there is not enough food produced to feed everyone. More jobs need to be created if Kenya is to make progress in the future.

Kenya Word Search
Page 110

1. Kilimanjaro
2. agriculture
3. wildlife
4. Kenyatta
5. Highland
6. harambee
7. Turkana
8. Swahili
9. Somalia
10. Nairobi
11. giraffe
12. equator
13. English
14. Britain
15. MauMau
16. Indian
17. coffee
18. Tsavo
19. Masai
20. maize
21. Arabs
22. Tana

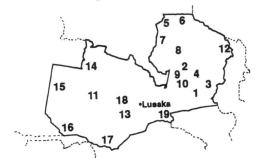

Zambia
Investigations
Page 111

1. Zaire, Angola, Namibia, Botswana, Zimbabwe, Malawi, Mozambique, and Tanzania
2. copper
3. Victoria Falls

Zambian Customs and Courtesies
Page 113

1. Unannounced visitors are not usually invited to share the host's meal
2. A knife, fork, and spoon are used to eat. Men, women, and children usually sit at the same table.
3. Institutions are for a large number of elderly people.
4. A family typically is comprised of only one or two children.
5. Girls marry late and dating is common before marriage.
6. It is not usually disrespectful to point at someone.
7. Kneeling is not a custom.
8. Most Americans want to affect the future, and they are assertive in their relationships.
9. Television is the main form of entertainment.
10. People are expected to be punctual.

Zambia Tourist Map
Page 114

South Africa
Investigations
Page 115

1. Kruger National Park
2. Nelson Mandela
3. gold

This Is South Africa
Page 117

1. M
2. L
3. J
4. K
5. N
6. P
7. B
8. O
9. A
10. C
11. H
12. E
13. F
14. G
15. D
16. I

Black South African Leaders
Page 118

1. Nelson Mandela was imprisoned for 27 years by the South African government for his early efforts against apartheid. After he was released from prison, he was elected president of the African National Congress, and he continues to struggle for change.
2. Bishop Desmond Tutu is the spiritual leader of about 2 million Anglicans, both blacks and whites. He won the Nobel Peace Prize for his commitment to peace. He continues to work to bring justice to his country.
3. Mangosuthu Buthelezi is the leader of the Inkatha Freedom Party. Buthelezi has fought white minority rule, but his followers, who are mostly members of the Zulu nation, have clashed with members of the African National Congress, resulting in thousands of deaths.

Latin America
Mexico
Investigations
Page 121

1. Aztec
2. President Carlos Salinas de Gortari
3. silver

Mexican Matchup
Page 123

1. F
2. N
3. L
4. H
5. M
6. G
7. A
8. C
9. J
10. B
11. E
12. K
13. I
14. R
15. P
16. O
17. Q
18. D

The Aztec-Chocolate Connection
Page 124

1. gods
2. Quetzalcoatl
3. plant
4. wisdom
5. drink
6. wealthy
7. cacao
8. valuable
9. money
10. Spaniards
11. 1519
12. Hernando Cortés
13. Spain
14. Europe
15. cacao
16. Ivory Coast, Brazil, Ghana Malaysia, and Nigeria are all acceptable answers.

Guatemala
Investigations
Page 125

1. marimba
2. Mayans
3. Quetzal

Guatemalan Culture
Page 127

1.	Mayans	9.	clothing
2.	Indian	10.	mestizos
3.	villages	11.	Spanish
4.	fields	12.	towns
5.	family	13.	cities
6.	textiles	14.	Spanish
7.	masks	15.	Catholic
8.	corn	16.	rituals

Mayan Civilization
Page 128

1. Priests, Stone masons, artists, and craft people lived in the city. Mayan farmers lived near the city.
2. Priests, and perhaps one chief priest, ruled the people.
3. The Mayans believed in many gods, including gods for corn, rain, and the sun.
4. Some occupations included religious leaders, stone masons, painters, sculptors, potters, jewelers, architects, and farmers.
5. The Mayans shaped the stone buildings with stone tools.

Costa Rica
Investigations
Page 129

1. 19,575 square miles
2. Oscar Arias Sanchez
3. Each star represents one of Costa Rica's seven provinces

Costa Rica Travel Brochure
Page 131

Answers will vary

Going Places in Costa Rica
Page 132

1.	G	8.	D
2.	B	9.	E
3.	N	10.	A
4.	I	11.	H
5.	K	12.	F
6.	M	13.	L
7.	O	14.	J
		15.	C

Peru
Investigations
Page 133

1. Incas
2. llama
3. anaconda

Peru's Geography
Page 135

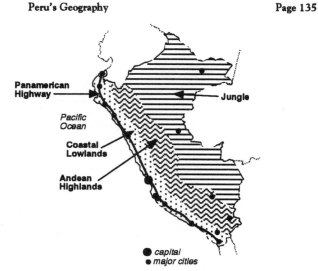

Peru From Top to Bottom
Page 136

Chile
Investigations
Page 137

1. Easter Island
2. Santiago
3. Tierra del Fuego

Chilean Economic Profile
Page 139

1. 13,286,000 (1991 Est.)
2. fifth
3. 292,257
4. 30%
5. copper, other minerals, foodstuffs, fish processing
6. wheat, potatoes, corn, onions, beans, fruit
7. copper, industrial products
8. Santiago, Vina del Mar, Valparaiso, Talcahuano

Chile's Liberator
Page 140

Answers will vary.

Brazil
Investigations
Page 141

1. 2.3 million square miles
2. *Christ the Redeemer*
3. Brasilia

Dateline Brazil
Page 143

M	D	H	K	E	J	A	C	F	I	N	B	G	L
1500	1519	1532-1548	1555	1624	1693	1722	1763	1808	1822	1888	1875-1915	1956	1969

Brazil's Geography
Page 144

1.	H	8.	K
2.	N	9.	I
3.	A	10.	G
4.	B	11.	J
5.	F	12.	M
6.	D	13.	L
7.	C		

Argentina
Investigations
Page 145

1. Buenos Aires
2. gauchos
3. Andes Mountains

Argentina's Land and People   Page 147

Northern Argentina	Cran Chaco, hard wood forest, Mesopotamia, humid, rolling plains
Pampa	fertile plains, gauchos
Andine	Puna, Piedmont, Mt. Aconcagua, skiing, lakes, Andes Mountains
Patagonia	dry, Colorado River, Tierra del Fuego, poor soil

Argentine Crossword   Page 148

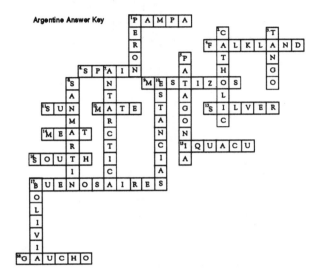

Argentine Answer Key

Uruguay

Investigations   Page 149
1. Argentina and Brazil
2. sheep
3. A water passage formed where seawater meets a river

Uruguay Trackdown   Page 151
1. Oriental Republic of Uruguay
2. latitude 34.52 South, longitude 56.12 West
3. 68,037 square miles
4. Temperate
5. Jose Gervasio Artigas
6. $2,970
7. wheat
8. hides and leather goods
9. 3,121,000
10. Spanish
11. because of the sandy beaches
12. Carrasco
13. estancias
14. European
15. National, Colorado

Mapping Uruguay   Page 152

Northern America
The United States of America

Investigations   Page 155
1. South Dakota
2. 1800
3. Out of many, one

State Flags   Page 157

1.	Louisiana	12.	Virginia
2.	Wyoming	13.	Kentucky
3.	Oklahoma	14.	South Dakota
4.	California	15.	Wisconsin
5.	New Hampshire	16.	Washington
6.	Maryland	17.	Hawaii
7.	New Mexico	18.	Mississippi
8.	South Carolina	19.	Nevada
9.	Rhode Island	20.	Tennessee
10.	Colorado	21.	Indiana
11.	Alabama	22.	Delaware
		23.	Alaska

America's Multiethnic Society   Page 158
1. white
2. 187,500,000
3. Native American/Eskimo
4. 22,500,000
5. 30,000,000
6. Hispanic
7. Asian-Pacific Island
8. Hispanic
9. Answers will vary, but should accurately reflect the ethnic composition of the U.S. displayed on the pie graph.

Canada

Investigations   Page 159
1. Newfoundland
2. Royal Canadian Mounted Police
3. Eskimo

Canada's Provinces and Territories   Page 161

1.	L	10.	K
2.	B	11.	A
3.	G	12.	B
4.	I	13.	E
5.	H	14.	J
6.	J	15.	G
7.	G	16.	B
8.	C	17.	G
9.	D	18.	F

Canadian Word Search   Page 162

1.	parliamentary	8.	remember	15.	Ottawa
2.	St Lawrence	9.	liberal	16.	nickel
3.	Vancouver	10.	village	17.	Jasper
4.	newsprint	11.	Trudeau	18.	beaver
5.	maple leaf	12.	Pearson	19.	Metis
6.	Macdonald	13.	English	20.	Logan
7.	Canada Day	14.	Quebec		

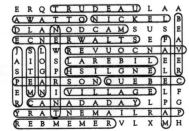

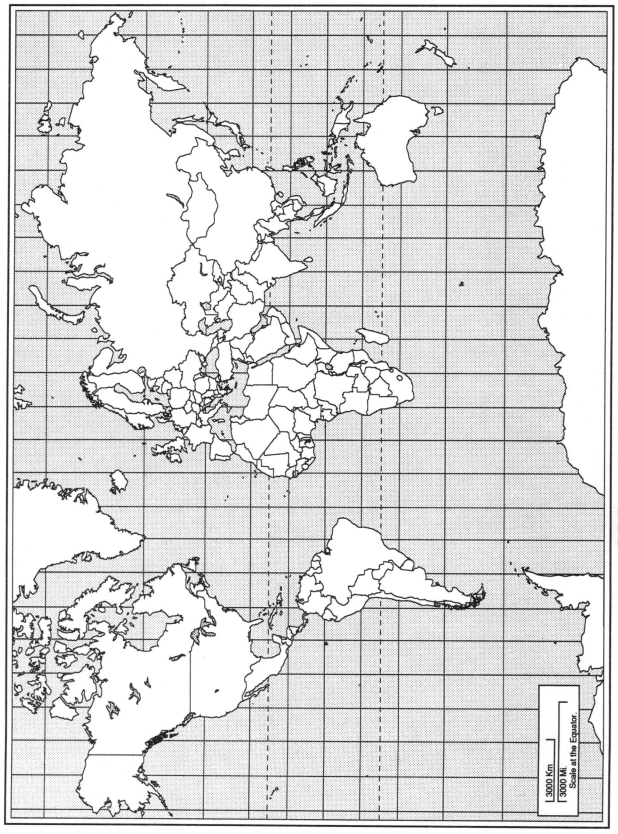

World Map

3000 Km
3000 Mi.
Scale at the Equator.

172